MY LIFE AS A MAINE-IAC

My Life as a Maine-iac

Muriel Young

Puckerbrush Press, Orono, Maine

ACKNOWLEDGEMENTS

Drawings on pages 9, 39, 81, 107, 125, 135, 169, 195 reproduced, with permission, from *Weathervanes and Whirligigs* by Ken Fitzgerald (Clarkson N. Potter, Inc., distributed by Crown Publishers, 1967).

Sketch of church on page 9 reproduced with permission of copyright holder, Security Savings Systems, Inc., New Cumberland, Pennsylvania.

Drawing of Indian on page 79 by Caroline Goodall.

Printed in the United States of America
by Howland's Printing Company, Old Town, Maine
Bound by University of Maine at Orono Press

*For Mother, and in warm appreciation
of my friends in the University
town of Orono, Maine*

Contents

Chapter 1

Life as a Maine-iac.

The Captain's voice came over the inter-com of the Jumbo Jet airplane. 'Ladies and gentlemen. We are now over Maine, and will be making our descent to Bangor in a few minutes. Will you fasten your safety belts, please?'

With a sense of mounting excitement I did so, and gazed through the plane's small window, hoping to catch a glimpse of the land-scape of the American State which was to be my home for the next few years. Soon we were below the clouds, and there, lying far below, was a vast, dark green carpet, interspersed here and there with large patches and ribbons of blue. This was Maine, the extreme North-Eastern State of America.

This was not my first visit to Maine. Three years before, my husband, a non-conformist minister in London, had exchanged churches with a young American pastor from Brewer, a town near Bangor, in central Maine. Although the snow had never left the ground during the whole five months we were there, the warmth and kindness of the people in the Congregational church in Brewer, more than made up for the often sub-zero temperatures. Now my husband had been invited to be minister of a Community church (one incorporating several denominations) in the town of Orono, which is about eight miles from Bangor. We had been at churches

9

in Essex, Cheshire and London over a period of twenty-eight years. Now we were starting a new task, in what was to be, I felt sure, our most stimulating and challenging of all, an American pastorate.

It is often said that life begins at forty. However, in my case I feel it really began at the age of fifty, when we left our London parish and came to live in Orono. In the old days, grandmothers used to sit by the fire, knitting, and wearing dark dresses, with lacy caps on their heads. Instead, here I was, embarking on a new way of life — a new adventure, meeting new and interesting people, and doing new and fascinating things.

The plane landed smoothly, and I was soon in the attractive new air-port lounge (on my previous visit it had been a very temporary, shack-like building) where I was greeted warmly by my husband, who had preceded me two months earlier. Then we were driving away from the air-port, past the noted McDonald's restaurant (famed for their hamburgers), and soon we were on a motorway, broad and tree-lined with dark green conifers. It was not long before we were entering the town of Orono, which I had seen only in photographs. We travelled slowly along Main Street with its typical white, wooden, New England houses, spick and span and freshly painted — a beautiful tree-lined road. We came eventually to a dazzling white wooden church with a steeple. This was it — the church I was to be part of, to grow to love so dearly. At the side of the church was a steepish hill, sign-posted Juniper Street. This we descended slowly, and there, at the foot of the hill, stood a large, square, reddish brown house surrounded by woodland. This was the Parsonage. I loved it at first sight, and even more when I entered. The church members had worked for months to prepare it for us, and it all looked absolutely beautiful. Every room had been freshly painted in attractive pastel shades, pine floors gleamed with a mirror-like sheen, wall papers had been tastefully chosen, and an elegant chandelier hung in the dining room. My own familiar furniture, which had just arrived from England, had been carefully arranged, and looked as though it really belonged there. After my long and tiring journey I felt too overwhelmed to say much, but I felt deeply moved at this obvious demonstration of love and care with which my new home had been prepared to welcome me.

After a quick wash and freshen-up (it was now well past midnight by my watch, though only about seven, American time) I was whisked off to a small welcoming reception at the home of one of the members of the Search Committee. The task of the Search Committee had been, over a period of two years, to interview and select a prospective new minister. It was a suggestion of the minister with whom we had had the exchange three years previously, which resulted in an invitation to my husband to spend a week in Orono in order to meet all the church groups and Committees, and to conduct the Sunday service. The whole visit was a great success, and an immediate rapport was established. We discovered later that one thing had mystified them a little. Whilst speaking to the Fellowship Circle, a group of pretty young women, my husband had referred to them as a 'nice homely group.' Homely, to Americans, we discovered, means 'plain and uncomely', not as we English mean by it, 'warm and friendly.' However, in spite of this, the morning after his return to England, a cable arrived issuing a warm, unanimous invitation to be the pastor of the church. So began the new adventure, and a new sphere of service in America.

I entered the long, ranch-type home a trifle apprehensively. What if they didn't like me? What if I didn't fit into this new environment? My fears were soon dispelled as our hostess (and, as I was to learn, the indefatigible organizer of the Parsonage refurbishing) welcomed me warmly, and led me to a room where a group of about fourteen people were assembled. 'Welcome to Orono, Mrs Young,' they said, smiling kindly. I liked them immediately, and knew then and there that these friendly, sincere people would prove to be my best loved friends. How fortunate I was.

A few days later the ladies of the church gave a 'shower' for me. They knew that I had had to leave my pots and pans, cooking utensils, and all the housewife's usual paraphernalia behind in England. Apart from the enormous cost of transporting these things across the Atlantic, the electrical appliances would have been useless as the voltage is different. I entered the church door and went down the stairs into the vestry, a large room below the church. Masses of blossom and lilacs were everywhere, on the staircase, in the vestibule. I entered the room to be confronted by rows of smiling faces, and a table stacked with beautifully wrapped, be-ribboned packages. Was this a mistake? Whose were all these gifts? I had never been to a 'shower' before, and didn't know quite what to expect. I was assured that they were all mine, and that I must open them all then and there. With trembling, excited fingers I carefully opened each package, watched expectantly by the fifty to sixty ladies. There were towels, sets of bowls, pans, sheets, glass ware, casserole dishes, recipe books, folding garden chairs, an electric food mixer, an iron, a tea-pot (indispensable to an Englishwoman). Nothing had been missed. There was just everything I needed. I was speechless with the kindness, loving thought and generosity of it all.

On my first Sunday in Orono I walked into the light, sun-filled church. It has the beautiful simplicity which is common to most New England churches. The walls are a pale cream, the pews a deep purple, with dull gold carpeting on the floor. A plain wooden cross stands out against the plain cream wall facing the congregation. Soon two blue-gowned members of the Junior Choir entered solemnly, and with long tapers lit the candles which stood on the altar in silver candelabra. Then from the back of the church the blue-gowned choirs, Junior and Senior, processed down the aisle singing with the congregation the first hymn. The minister followed, and they all took their places in choir pews and pulpit respectively. The service began and seemed to follow a pattern very similar to that to which I had been accustomed since childhood. I felt 'at home' and accepted in our new pastorate.

I soon found that there were only a few shops in Orono — a drug store, a small supermarket, a florist's, a jeweller's, a hard-ware store, and that was about all. This was quite a contrast to our London pastorate with its abundance of stores and small shops. It soon became apparent that most of the shopping is done at the large precincts or malls which are situated outside the towns, and some of these have sixty to ninety stores all under one roof. Their huge parking areas cater for thousands of customers, some of whom come hundreds of miles from remote parts of the State and from Canada.

Orono is a typical New England town, its Main Street flanked by well-kept, dignified white wooden houses. It is a friendly town, with warm, out-going people. A large proportion of Orono's population is employed in some capacity at the University of Maine at Orono. The campus of the University is extensive, and during term time the town overflows with the students, and life revolves around the University and its activities. Orono was first settled by Jeremiah Colburn and Joshua Ayers in 1774, just one year before the Revolution. Both men brought their families, and Colburn built his log cabin near what is now Orono's shopping area, while Ayers built his cabin in the area of the street in which we now live. The same year they built together a mill, near the mouth of the Stillwater River, and gradually the community began to grow and expand. Growth continued slowly, and by 1820 the population of Orono was still only 415. Throughout this time the plantation had no doctor, lawyer, or settled minister. There were no churches, roads were rough tracks, and most of the homes were of a very humble kind. The only industry was lumbering.

Several place names were used in the area before it became Orono. For a long time the Penobscot Indians had a camping ground or small village in the area, and many artifacts and other relics were found by the early settlers. The Indian name for this camping ground is unknown, but a nearby place was called Arumsunk-hungan, or more accurately, according to an authority on Indian names, Nahum-sunk-hungan, meaning 'alewife fishing place below the outlet.' The Stillwater River they called Skit-i-kuk, which was their usual term for 'dead water on a stream.' The English settlers seem to have called the river, Deadwater, until Owen Madden, a school teacher in Orono and Bangor in the early pioneer days, decided that the name Stillwater had a much more pleasant sound. Orono village was once known as Stillwater, until on March 12th, 1806, the General Court of Massachusetts passed an Act 'to incorporate the Plantation heretofore called Stillwater into a town by the name of Orono.'

In his *History of Maine*, 1832, Judge William D. Williamson, the noted Maine historian, wrote, 'It is the 162nd town in the State of Maine, taking its name from a distinguished chief of the Penobscot tribe, whose friendship to the cause of American liberties gave him an elevated place in the public estimation.' Orono is the only town in Maine which bears the name of an Indian chief. There are Indian names for lakes, rivers, mountains and towns, such as Megunticook, Piscataquis, Chemquassabumtook, Mattawamkeag, and hundreds of others. A monument stands on the Main Street of Orono, next to the Catholic church. This plinth of rough stone was erected to the memory of this well-loved chief. The inscription on it reads 'Erected in memory of Joseph Orono, Catholic Indian chief.'

When I arrived in Orono in May, a Winter had just ended. I realised very soon that Spring is an extremely short season in Maine, and that almost overnight the temperatures can change from the 30's to the 80's, in fact from Winter almost immediately into Summer.

The Parsonage stands in a wild, wooded area which seems to abound in wild life. One bright morning in June I glanced out of the window and saw what appeared to be an over-sized guinea-pig sitting up on its haunches, absolutely immobile, and staring fixedly in front of it, perhaps hoping it couldn't be seen. I learned that this was a wood-chuck (or ground hog), quite a harmless animal, but with an insatiable appetite for garden produce, so that they are not popular. Frogs, too, of all shapes, sizes and colours, seem to be everywhere, croaking noisily in the dusk, while fire flies (or lightning bugs) glimmer among the trees in the Summer evenings. One September evening, after I had put out the trash bin for collection the next morning, I heard a clatter on the porch outside. Going to investigate, I saw in the dim light, at the foot of the steps, a creature with a pointed, fox-like snout, with black markings around its eyes, making it appear as though it were wearing a mask, and a striped, bushy tail. It made no attempt to move — but I did, hastily. The next morning trash was littered everywhere, orange peel, paper, banana skins, chicken bones. As I started to clear up the mess, the mail man arrived in his little blue jeep. 'I see you've had visitors,' he said cheerily. 'You've got raccoons down in that gully,' and he pointed toward the wild, wooded area at the back of the parsonage. Another night in early Autumn, we heard the sound of something heavy falling on the back porch. Hurrying to see what the cause of the noise might be, we turned on the outside light and looked out of the glass door. The trash bin had been pulled over, and there, busily dragging out the refuse, were not one, not two, but five sleek, well-fed raccoons. Looking up boldly at our astonished faces this completely fearless group made no attempt at all to leave, but with their incredibly tiny, long clawed paws, went on busily sorting and tearing at the contents of the bin. After this, we purchased a stout strap, which fastened securely over the top of the trash bin. Somehow, though, I felt strangely guilty for so depriving our scavengers of further feasts.

Unfortunately, I have not seen a live Maine bear, though they live in the forests, and can be seen occasionally around town refuse dumps. Bears are hunted in the hunting season in the Fall, and I once saw one hanging from a tree, and was sad to know that it had not been allowed to live and roam, wild and free. One of our church members had a young bear wandering around her garden one day. She informed the police and it was captured and taken back to a forest near the town. The Maine black bear is the University of Maine's mascot. Apparently it is quite harmless unless it is attacked, and I feel it should be protected and not allowed to become extinct because of indiscriminate hunting. On many occasions I have been very aware of the proximity of a skunk. Its acrid, revolting odour is unmistakable, and I have no desire to make a closer acquaintance. Hordes of grey squirrels gambol around the Parsonage, swing on the trees, and jump on to the roof. Sometimes they peer cheekily through our bedroom window. One dull wintry morning, whilst dusting, I happened to glance out of the window, and saw, to my amazement, a dark, black shape climbing slowly up a fir tree in my neighbour's garden. Excitedly I called my husband. Was it a bear? It certainly looked like one. We called the police, who came within a few minutes. At first they couldn't see anything, and I hoped they wouldn't think it was an illusion on my part. However, soon one of them called out, 'There it is!' At the top of a tall tree was a huge, dark round ball. 'Gee, that's not a bear, Ma'am, that's a porcupine. A big 'un, too.' Well, it was not the bear I had hoped for, but after all, how many people have ever seen a porcupine at the top of a fir tree?

Maine birds are really beautiful and abundant. The blue jay with its lovely plumage and harsh cry is very prevalent around the Parsonage. Each year the phoebes, with their plaintive call, build their nests in a corner of our front porch. I never mind the mess they make, but am fearful always for their safety. There are a great number of very crafty cats along our street, who skulk constantly behind the trees and bushes surrounding the house, ready to pounce. There are, too, the yellow grosbeaks, the little nuthatch, the red-winged blackbird, the tiny, darting humming bird, and the little black-capped chickadee (which is Maine's State bird). On the lakes, the eerie wail of the loon can be heard over the water. The American bald eagle is becoming rare, but some fortunate people have seen it along the Penobscot River. I have only once seen the red cardinal. Its scarlet plumage was beautiful, standing out against the whiteness of the snow, as it made a rare appearance in search of food after a Winter storm.

A short time after my arrival in Orono, I decided, one day, to attempt a bit of weeding in a particularly untidy part of the garden. It was then that I discovered the black flies for which Maine is noted, or rather, I should say that they discovered me. Within seconds I was surrounded by hordes of these small, vindictive flies. I worked steadily for a couple of hours, determined to ignore them if possible. I was perspiring profusely in the 85 degree temperature, and swiped wildly at the persistent swarm of tiny black monsters, as they hovered lovingly and determinedly around my head. To my horror, when I went inside at last and peered into the mirror, I saw scores of flies adhering to my damp skin. Within a short time I began to look like a prize-fighter. My ears were swollen to at least three times their normal size, my cheeks inflamed and puffed out like a hamster's, and my eyelids had swollen so much that there remained only narrow slits through which I could peep and see the havoc which my unwelcome guests had caused.

Was this grotesque, hideous face I could barely see really mine? The doctor I visited sympathized and gave me an injection, and the suggestion that I should make a paste of meat tenderizer and water, and place this on the bites. This sounded and looked rather odd, but really did take away the awful irritation and swelling, and gradually I returned to normality. These flies have become the bane of my life, and are around to bother me from June until September. There is something about me which they seem to love, and as soon as I make an appearance the entire black fly population seems to rise and zero in on me, as if the signal goes out, 'Fee-fi-fo-fum, we smell the blood of an English*woman*.' Not all people react as violently as I do to their sting, and I am told one builds up a resistance to the little monsters after a time. How long, I wonder?

I read a very informative article on this horrid little pest, which described the black fly as a tiny, vicious, blood-sucking insect that attacks in swarms and causes indescribable discomfort. It seems that far more than being a mere annoyance, black flies are capable of killing cattle, sheep, fowl, horses, and even humans. It has large eyes, short legs, a humped back, and broad gauzy wings, and measures just slightly larger than the tip of a ball point pen. The present major biting species in Maine produces only one generation, which begins mating as soon as it emerges from its cocoon-like chrysalis in late Spring and early Summer. After mating, the female lays many hundreds of eggs, but these eggs remain inactive for almost a year until the following Spring, when they develop into larvae, and subsequently into more black flies, which immediately begin their mating for the following year's generation. It is the egg laying process that is responsible for the vicious and dangerous characteristics of the female black fly, for it is she alone who does the biting. Jeffrey Granett, research Assistant Professor in the Department of Entomology at the University of Maine at Orono, says, 'In order for the eggs to be laid, female black flies must obtain a meal by biting a warm blooded creature. The blood serves as a necessary protein source for development of the eggs.' The black fly, apparently, does not 'bite' at all. It chews a hole in its victim, ruptures the tiny blood vessels in the area, and applies an anti-coagulant saliva to keep the wound from healing while it drinks the needed blood. In some humans, black fly bites cause an extreme allergic reaction that requires immediate medical attention, and have been known to cause death.

It seems that in certain areas of Maine turkeys cannot be raised commercially because of their vulnerability to black fly bites. It is ironic that as Maine moves ahead in its programme to clean up its streams and rivers, it is inadvertently greatly expanding its black fly population. Water cleanliness is essential to the black fly, for the larvae will not live and develop in polluted water. It needs fast running, clean water for its development. Over the years scientists and woodsmen have studiously noticed the behaviour and certain traits of the black fly. They advise that an upright person is more likely to attract flies than one lying flat on or near the ground. Obviously one should lie low. It seems, too, that dark colours attract them more than light ones, that they attack mainly in daylight hours, and never when a high wind is blowing. An approaching storm makes them particularly blood-thirsty, and there are often massive attacks. An old Mainer offered his own brand of self-protection. He said, 'When a swarm of them black flies moves in on you, there's just one thing to do, and that is to get out of there fast, even if you have to duck into your camp, or even jump into the water. You'll never win against them unless you can kill them all — and that ain't ever been done yet.'

The first Summer passed slowly and gave us time to become acclimatized and to get to know the unusual and beautiful State which was now our home. One day the telephone rang. It was one of our church members. 'Hi, there,' he said. 'We're out at our camp at Eddington Pond. Why don't you come out tomorrow, stay the night, and spend the next day with us? Be sure to wear casual clothes.' We thanked him, said we'd love to come, and asked for directions. The next day was beautiful, and suitably attired in blue jeans, check shirts and sneakers, we set off. The camp was only about sixteen miles from Orono, just off the main road. Following the directions we had been given, we looked out for a red barn on the left hand side of the road, with a rough path immediately opposite. Following the rough path for about one hundred yards we came suddenly upon a yellow and white painted cottage set among the trees. A few steps further and we were in the open. There before us was a vast expanse of shimmering deep blue water. This was Eddington Pond, a beautiful lake fringed with trees and dotted along the shores with small unobtrusive cabins or cottages. To come upon this lovely spot so suddenly and unexpectedly, so near a main road, was quite astonishing.

Our host and hostess greeted us warmly, looking relaxed and happy. After swinging on the porch hammock, sipping iced tea, and enjoying the idyllic scene before us for a while, our hostess said, 'While I prepare supper, off you go in the canoe for half an hour.' Our host readied the canoe, which looked rather light and flimsy to me, and handed us a life-jacket and a paddle each. 'Off you go,' he laughed as I looked rather apprehensive. I had never been in a canoe before, and didn't know what to do with the paddle. After a shaky start we soon learned how to push back the water and keep to the same rhythm, and soon were gliding swiftly and certainly along the lake, which is about three quarters of a mile long, and about half a mile wide. (Eddington Pond is one of the smaller of Maine's more than two thousand lakes, and is therefore called a pond.) We returned to the camp about half an hour later, exhilarated, invigorated, and more than satisfied at our progress in our first canoeing venture. We clambered ashore, to be greeted by the mouth-watering aroma of clam chowder, hamburgers, blueberry pie and coffee, all typical Maine fare. What could be more perfect? Our expedition had given us quite an appetite. We sat in the dusk on the porch, eating and gazing out at the lake — the silence broken only by the eerie lament of a loon out on the water. Soon it was time for bed, and we ascended the steep staircase from the one living-room with its enormous stone fireplace, to an equally large, loft-like area above it. The large and comfortable mattress was very inviting after our unaccustomed exercise, and we were soon asleep.

The next morning we awoke to. a dazzling scene, a beautiful day, and the aroma of coffee, scrambled eggs and toast. The lake shimmered in the sunshine, the sky was a vivid blue, clear and cloudless, the air was like champagne, vital and stimulating. It was a day when one was truly thankful to be alive. After breakfast we all set out in a rowing boat to explore the lake. A large muskrat swam lazily beside the boat. In the rushes wild duck squawked noisily, and flapped their wings as they fled from our unwelcome intrusion of their privacy. I dabbled my hands in the clear water and plucked some white water lilies as we passed. A large bull frog croaked raucously from a lily pad. It was fascinating to see the intricately built beaver dams, and to observe the wild life in these lovely surroundings. Later we returned to the cottage and enjoyed a leisurely swim in the lake. Not until afterwards did our host mention casually that there were snapping turtles in the lake, or my swim would have been far less leisurely and complacent. Feeling refreshed and cool, we then set off in a truck to the top of a mountain named Black Cap. We went bumping up and up along a rough track. I sat in the back of the truck in my blue jeans, check shirt and sneakers, thinking this was a far cry from our London parish with the city streets and conventional clothes. We reached the top at last, breathed in the freshness and loveliness of it all, and feasted our eyes on the panorama which stretched below and around us. There was no house in sight — no other human — just a vast carpet of dark green conifers interspersed with the brilliant, sparkling patches of blue lakes. As I gazed over this serenity the words of Martin Luther King's last speech in Memphis before his assassination sprang suddenly into my mind: 'I have been to the mountain top. I have looked over and seen the promised land.'' Wc came down from the mountain feeling renewed and a little awed by the untouched beauty. We left the cottage reluctantly to return to Orono. A lot had been packed into that day and a half, and we felt we were really beginning to know and love Maine.

Another day on a crisp Fall evening, we had been invited to spend a few hours at the Summer cottage of two other church members before they closed it for the Winter. The log cabin was about thirty miles from Orono, and stood on a high point above the sea. A log fire was burning in the stone fire-place, and our host outlined our programme for the evening. We were going for a tramp through the woods, then going to dig for clams, and then take a boat trip to see the seals on the rocks nearby. We would return for supper. The walk was invigorating on the springy turf of the forest floor, the air crisp and cool. On the beach we dug deeply for clams in the blackish mud, and soon had a sizeable pile. Leaving these in a pail, we set off for the boat trip, exhilarated as the wind and spray beat on our faces. It was not long before we saw the seals, their large grey shapes lying lazily on the rocks ahead of us. At our approach they all slithered noiselessly into the grey water. Back at the cabin, we basked contentedly in front of the blazing log fire, whilst our hostess set to work cooking the clams we had just dug. Within a short time we ate them, dripping with butter, and they were succulent and sweet.

After this, steaks were grilled over the wood fire, and these, too, we devoured hungrily with salad. Nothing had ever tasted so good. Our outdoor activities had given us quite an appetite. After the meal and some stimulating conversation we returned to Orono by moonlight.

We had become familiar with Maine's rock-bound coast and many of the little fishing harbours with their little weathered houses with lobster pots outside. We had visited several of Maine's numerous lakes, too, but so far had not visited the area of Northern Maine and Mount Katahdin, of which we had heard so much. However, this we planned to do.

Katahdin, rising massive and inscrutable to an altitude of 5,267 feet, dominates the lakes and forests of Northern Maine, and for hundreds of years was honoured as the dwelling place of the sacred spirits of the Abenaki Indians. The Maine author Fannie Hardy Eckstorm (1881-1946) was a knowledgeable source of the legends of Mount Katahdin. She believed that at least three different Indian concepts were covered by the Indian word 'bumole' or 'Pamola' to the white man. One was Wuchowsen, the spirit of the night wind, whom an old Indian woman described as having 'no body, all legs, hands.' Wuchowsen created the breezes by flapping his wings, and was considered harmless. A second concept was the Storm-bird. This was a huge, bird-like creature with fearsome beak and claws, and a head as large as four horses. In his best mood this creature was nasty, and when aroused to anger, which was often, he used his considerable power to create violent winds and devastating snowstorms. The legends of the Storm-bird concerned his attempts to keep men from climbing Katahdin. Indians and white men alike were safe from his wrath if they stayed below the tree-line. If they climbed any higher, however, they could expect no mercy. Pamola used high winds, fog, and snowstorms to keep his mountaintop home free from intruders. A

well known legend of such an incident was of the famous
Penobscot chief, John Neptune, who went hunting on
the mountain, and spent the night there in a shack with
a strong door. Enraged at Neptune's temerity at invading
his territory, Pamola came swooping down from his
stronghold to destroy him. He hammered on the door, he
roared and blew, but to no avail. Pamola finally stormed
away, and the next day Neptune descended the mountain
safely. The third concept was human in form. It was
gigantic, majestic, with stony eyebrows and cheekbones.
This Spirit of Katahdin lived inside the mountain with his
Indian wife and children, and showed a friendly concern
for the Indians.

By the 1830's and 40's lumbering operations in the area
of Katahdin had begun in earnest, and went on until
the Great Northern Paper Company's last major operations of 1922 and 1923. By the 1890's a group of Bangor
citizens were proposing the creation of a game preserve,
and it was suggested in 1895 that a thirty square mile
area surrounding Katahdin should become a State Park.
Eventually, after decades of tenacious and sustained
effort, it was Percival Baxter, son of a wealthy Portland
businessman, and, later, Governor of Maine, who created
by his own individual efforts what is now Baxter State
Park. In 1930, Baxter persuaded the Great Northern
Paper Company to sell him a tract of 5,960 acres, which
included most of Katahdin. The next year he deeded
these lands to the State for use as a park, with the stipu-
lation that the area should 'forever be used for public
park and recreational purposes, forever left in its natural
wild state, forever be kept as a sanctuary for wild beasts
and birds, that no roads or ways for motor vehicles
shall hereafter be constructed thereon or therein.'
Baxter determined to increase the size of the park to as
much as 200,000 acres, and to provide financially for
long-term operation. This he achieved, and over a period
of thirty years purchased and subsequently bequeathed
in trust, parcels of land around and including Mount

Katahdin. The 200,000 acres were to belong to the people of Maine. Percival Baxter wanted man to enjoy the area simply and naturally without bringing in the paraphernalia of technological civilization with its noise and confusion. Campers, trailers, motor cycles are not allowed to pass through the gates, there are dirt roads, simple and basic cabins, and no souvenir stands. The staff of thirteen permanent wardens and twenty seven seasonal employees make sure that Baxter's wishes are carried out, and that his park remains 'forever wild.'

It was a lovely July morning when we set out with two friends for our first visit to Baxter State Park. After a four-hour-long journey by car from Orono, stopping only for a meal, and in order to purchase necessary food supplies at a large supermarket, we arrived at the entrance of the park. After signing in at the Warden's post we drove on through the forest to find our cabins at Daicey Pond. Clustered around the lake's edge there were just six cabins. Ours was number three, and bore the name Vat 95, and was situated a few feet from the edge of the lake. Immediately opposite, across the lake, Mount Katahdin stood, lofty and awe-inspiringly beautiful in the afternoon sunshine. The cabin was of rough logs, constructed in the way the early settlers might have done. It was simple and basic, and to me, most romantic. There was a bed, a rough chest, a wooden table on which stood a bowl and jug, a gas mantle, a wood-stove in one corner, and that was it. A notice was pinned to the wall saying that all water must be boiled (as this had to be drawn from the lake). We quickly settled in, making up the beds with the bedding we had brought, and unpacking our few clothes. This done, we then went to the cabin of our friends, which was close by, though at a higher level, in a more wooded area. A wood-fire was already blazing outside the cabin, and there was the delicious aroma of steaks grilling, whilst on the picnic table a large bowl of salad stood invitingly, together with rolls and butter and fruit. Food had never tasted so wonderful as it did in that clear, pure air, and in that truly magnificent setting. I felt at peace with the world. Surely, I thought, this is how life ought to be.

Soon it became dusk, and then a change came over the scene. It began to rain heavily and there was the distant roll of thunder. Soon lightning streaked across the sky and the rain drummed incessantly on the roof of the cabin. We decided to call it a day, and retired to our own cabin, stumbling in the dark over the roots of trees, and fumbling for the latch of the cabin door in the sudden inky blackness of the forest night. The storm continued all night and sleep was fitful. I remembered the Indian legend of Pamola, whom they believed lived in the mountain. The Indians believed that when there was thunder and lightning, this was a sign that Pamola was angry. Perhaps the old legend was true and he was showing his displeasure at our presence. Eventually I managed to sleep, and awakened to the sound of birds twittering. I drew aside the curtains, and there, a few feet away, was the lake shimmering in the bright sunlight, with Katahdin shrouded in swirling mist which was rapidly clearing. Ah, it looked as though Pamola was happy today. I dressed hurriedly and went outside to breathe in the pure, intoxicating freshness of the air, and to drink in the beauty of the scene before me. From the direction of our friends' cabin there was an inviting scent of wood smoke, too, and coffee, and best of all, bacon cooking.

We spent three heavenly days, just sitting and soaking up the sunshine, the beauty and the peace, eating in the open air some of the best meals I have ever tasted, watching the fascinating little chipmunks greedily devour the nuts we left for them, and canoeing on the lake. All too soon it was time for us to pack up our belongings, clean the cabin and leave it ready for the next visitors. The only slight disappointment I felt as we drove away through the park was that I had not seen a bear or a moose. Just as we were leaving the area just beyond the warden's post on the track leading to the exit gates, our friends in the preceding car beckoned us to stop. We obeyed, and they pointed to a pool by the side of the road. At the other side of the pool a large moose stood in the water, placidly eating some vegetation from the pool. He was a magnificent animal, huge, dark and sleek. The huge antlers were unwieldy and clumsy on his head, and the face long and rather comical. The moose gazed fearlessly and complacently at us, making no attempt to move, and we remained for a while regarding each other. This seemed to me to be the perfect ending to a most memorable experience.

During the long Summer vacation, Orono becomes almost deserted, with the students gone, and most of the town's inhabitants at their cabins or cottages on the shores of the lakes or at the coast. Therefore the church life comes more or less to a standstill from mid-June to the beginning of September. Most of our church members are Professors of the University and their families. The Director of Physical Education, athletics and football coaches, the Administrative staff — all serve the University in some capacity. At the beginning of September Orono suddenly comes alive again. Notices appear outside the banks and in the stores, 'Welcome back, U.M.O. students.' The streets fill with students, and cars with luggage piled high on roof-racks cram the parking areas and the roads leading to the University. The church starts on its energetic winter programme, with filled pews at Sunday services, lectures, suppers, meetings and other activities. Some September days become crisp and fresh, hinting subtly of change, and the squirrels become even busier, darting to and fro carrying nuts to their nests, their cheeks bulging with seeds and berries to be hoarded away for the oncoming winter. Suddenly the forests, valleys and mountainsides become streaked with flaming, glowing colour. Vivid bursts of gold, burgundy, crimson and tawny russet intermingle with the dark evergreens. Silhouetted against unbelievably clear, deep blue skies, the glory of Autumn in Maine is indescribable in its beauty. Soon the last colour fades and the roads are showered with falling leaves. The forests take on a subtler contrast — the dark green conifers stand beside the grey leafless trees, while brown leaves cover the forest floor. At the end of October huge orange pumpkins appear on the front porches of houses, ready for Hallowe'en. We buy a big supply of candy from the store ready for the 'trick or treaters' who arrive at our door throughout the evening of the last day of October. This is supposed to be the time when, if no treats are given, tricks are played on the household. Groups of children, some dressed as witches, others as ghosts or monsters, with weird masks on their faces, knock at the Parsonage door. We dole out the candy, hoping we have bought a sufficient quantity, and they depart gleefully with their spoils, some with pillow-cases bulging with 'goodies.' Many of these children are quite young, and we have been appalled to hear on the radio that in some areas children have been given apples with pieces of razor blades embedded in them, and candies containing harmful additives. Parents are warned not to let children go out 'trick or treating' unaccompanied. What a sad reflection on our times.

November is the hunting season in Maine, and the stores are filled with brilliant fluorescent red caps and jackets. These are worn so that the hunters can be clearly visible to each other. There have been quite a number of hunting fatalities when, in the distance, a hunter has been mistaken for an animal. Thanksgiving is, of course, one of the highlights of the year, a time of family reunions and celebration. There is always an Ecumenical service in Orono at Thanksgiving, when all the churches co-operate fully and congregate at the Catholic church, the town's largest. After what is always an inspiring service, everyone goes down to a hall below the church to meet together socially, and vast quantities of sandwiches, cookies and beverages are consumed. The ladies of each church take it in turn to prepare and serve the refreshments, and, believe me, it is no light task to cut sandwiches for over five hundred people.

One memorable Thanksgiving day we were asked to share the special meal at the home of some friends who own a blueberry farm at the top of a mountain surrounded by vast acres of forest land. Sun Top Farm is situated in a spectacular spot, and on this particular day it was even more so, as a blinding snow storm was raging. We drove up and up the rough track leading to the farm, making slow progress as it was hard to see through the windscreen. Our host had telephoned before we left home to say that if the going became too difficult, we must leave the car a mile or so from the farm, and telephone from his nearest neighbour. He would then come with a special truck to fetch us. However, we eventually managed to reach the top without help. Our friends hurried to the door to let us in, and we were soon seated before a blazing fire drinking hot punch. Looking out of the large picture window, as far as the eye could see there was nothing but dark green conifers, their branches capped with snow. A red barn loomed out against the swirling whiteness of the snow, and near the house several varieties of birds came boldly to the bird feeders as the storm raged on. Soon the family gathered at the table for the traditional Thanksgiving meal of turkey, cranberry sauce, sweet potatoes and squash. This was followed by pumpkin pie, and apple and mince tarts. After a time of warmth and conviviality, when we were made to feel really part of the family gathering, it was time to leave and to drive again through the storm to a wedding at Brewer, which was about ten miles away. Weddings often take place in the late afternoon, but this particular afternoon in late November, with a blizzard raging, seemed to be a rather bizarre time for one. However, after a hazardous tussle with the elements on our way to the church, we arrived there thankfully at last, and the weather was forgotten as we saw the radiant bride awaiting us.

The first Winter was the hardest. I had never seen so much snow, and as our house is at the bottom of a steep hill, it became a kind of icy ski slope on which it was almost impossible to move a step without falling headlong. One bitterly cold night before Christmas I set out on foot to go to the local school where I was to serve cocoa and cookies to a group of carol singers. I had gone only a few yards when my feet shot from under me, and as I put out a hand to steady myself, I felt a sharp, sudden pain in my wrist. I knew at once it was broken, and without stopping to think, rushed madly down the hill to the Parsonage — the hill down which I normally crept cautiously in such hazardous conditions. Miraculously I kept my footing, and reached the house safely. It was a wild, stormy night, and the radio was warning motorists not to venture out unless it was absolutely essential. In my case it obviously was. We travelled to the hospital slowly and carefully through the blinding snow-storm, the car slithering dangerously over the icy roads. At last we reached the hospital which was several miles away. The arm was X-rayed and the break confirmed. The surgeon was unfortunately not there but at another hospital a few miles away, so that there was a long wait before the arm could be set. In the meantime a group of male singers (a barber shop quartet) who were entertaining the patients with a pre-Christmas programme, stopped at the Emergency ward and sang several numbers. To say I was not in the mood just then for 'Happy days are here again' would have been an understatement. After what seemed an interminable time, the surgeon arrived, brushing the snow from his hair, and began to set the arm. As he was doing so he said, 'You're English, aren't you? Of course I suppose you realise that our Health Service is far superior to your National Health

Service.' I felt that this was probably neither the time nor the place to argue, and remained silent.

I soon found out how incapacitating it is to have only the use of one arm. My friends were wonderful, however, and arrived at the Parsonage door bearing containers of hot soup, casserole dishes, various kinds of bread and cookies, and all kinds of good things. When my husband broke a bone in his hand after a similar fall on the ice a week later, we were indeed at a disadvantage. One morning we were awakened by the regular 'clink - clink' of metal on the front path. We peered through the curtains to see a kind and capable woman neighbour digging determinedly and purposefully, to clear the path of ice and a new heavy snow-fall.

We have learned to live with the long cold Maine Winters, and to know that the cold is part of Maine — bracing, beautiful, challenging. In November the mornings are crisp, the trees silvered with frost, but we are prepared. Storm windows are fitted to every window of the Parsonage, every aperture is sealed against the searching cold. Snow tyres are fixed on the car. Snow shovels and sand are placed in readiness, and a good stock of logs stacked neatly in the wood-shed. We wear special boots and quilted nylon jackets, woollen gloves and caps, and to prevent slipping on the rock-hard, icy ground, metal spikes to strap over our boots. We are ready.

There are minor flurries at first, then as the air becomes gradually colder the skies become heavy and slate-grey. Soon the snow falls in big, soft flakes that blot out the sky. The temperature drops to below zero. Everything comes to a complete standstill for a time. No one ventures outside unless it is absolutely necessary — the roads become filled with the driving snow. Sometimes a snow-storm can beat on incessantly for a day and a night before ceasing reluctantly. The sun then can be blinding, and the sky a brilliant clear blue. Beneath the sun's rays the snow becomes a palish ice blue. Tall and graceful drifts of snow resemble canopies of alabaster. The dark green conifers have caps of fresh white snow on their branches. Other trees have their bare branches encrusted with gems of frost and snow that sparkle in the sunshine like a mantle of silver lace filigree. Icicles six feet long hang like crystal chandeliers from the eaves of the Parsonage. The whole countryside becomes a magical, dazzling world of white. Even the lakes and rivers stand in white frozen silence. An ice storm is even more spectacularly lovely. Occasionally in Winter there is an exceptionally heavy rainfall, and when this freezes, the trees' branches are encased in ice which glitters and sparkles in the sun's rays like crystals, diamonds and silver. Low bushes, shrubs, grass and undergrowth, all appear to be of spun glass, each blade of grass like a shining dagger.

Each day I walk along the deeply rutted, iron-hard road from the Parsonage to the grocery store a few hundred yards away. Scraped by the town's ploughs, the ground becomes as hard and unyielding as granite after months of built-up, solid ice. The metal spikes or 'creepers' I wear over my boots to grip the ice and prevent me from slipping, strike the ground noisily with each step I take, but at least I feel safe. My nostrils tense as the cold air pierces them. I walk more quickly, breathe more deeply, bracing my back against the searching cold, my woollen cap pulled well over my ears. The icy touch of the cold probes beneath my jacket and scarf with persistent fingers. Gradually, though, one becomes enlivened and glowing after walking in the clean, cold, intoxicating air. Winter is a time Maine people can enjoy as few others can. There is skiing, ice-skating, snow-shoeing, snowmobiling, cross-country skiing and ice fishing. One of the things I enjoy most in Winter are the ice hockey games which are held in the new arena at the University. The speed and excitement and boisterousness of the game, the dazzling white of the rink under the high-powered lights, the blaring brass band, all add up to a most exhilarating and enjoyable experience. I enjoy most the tussling of the players, the breaking of hockey sticks, the puck sometimes soaring high over the protective barrier into the crowd. I become a different person as I cheer on the 'Black Bears' and boo wholeheartedly as an opposing team member unfairly tackles one of ours.

At the beginning of December, at the Christmas workshop which is held in the large vestry beneath the church, there are scenes of great activity. Parents and children gather for a sandwich lunch, then everyone gets busy on one project or another. In one corner, colourful banners are made by cutting out motifs of stars and bells and other Christmas symbols of bright felt, and then glueing these on to a larger piece of contrasting coloured felt. A string is attached for hanging, and the finished product proudly admired. In another corner electric fret-saws buzz busily away, nails are hammered, and wood is sanded, as miniature sleighs are constructed. In yet another corner, under expert supervision, little fingers are sticky with coloured frosting as gingerbread men and cookies are decorated with holly and stars and other designs. Crumbs on small mouths bear witness of their having sampled their handiwork. Christmas tree decorations of moulded plaster are painted colourfully and then sprinkled with glitter dust of silver and gold. In the centre of the room the adults are busy. Boughs of fir, spruce and cypress surround them, and under expert tuition these are cut to the correct size, and bound neatly around a circle of wood or metal. Eventually, after much patience and trimming, a number of quite professional-looking Christmas wreaths emerge. These are then decorated with scarlet ribbon bows, and carried proudly home, where they are hung on the front doors of the houses. The church altar is banked with pots of brilliant scarlet poinsettias for the Christmas services. Outside the churches and banks, Christmas trees illumined with colourful lights brighten the darkened streets, and

brilliantly lighted snow-flakes hang overhead on the
lamp standards. From the windows of houses electric
candles of blue and red and gold shine invitingly and
warmly. Everywhere there is an air of expectancy and
good cheer. It is Christmas.

Since childhood I have always loved Amateur Dra-
matics, and have joined the drama group in every church.
To my disappointment, I found that there was not one at
the church at Orono, and no stage or facilities. I tentatively suggested as an Easter programme, a one-act
play for women. Everyone seemed very enthusiastic.
I carefully cast the play and we began rehearsing. The
play was well written, the cast spirited, but there were
no curtains, no proper exits and entrances, and so we
had to improvise. With a few potted palms and earthenware pots placed strategically around a wooden bench
or two, there was the courtyard. Utilizing the large
windows in the Parish house, the 'women of Jerusalem', in gaily coloured Eastern robes, peered through
from their secluded courtyard to the main road outside (now the main thoroughfare in Jerusalem). Dra-
matically they conveyed to the audience the exciting
events taking place in their city on that day. At the dress
rehearsal everything was rising to an exciting crescendo
as the 'women of Jerusalem' gasped in horror at the
sight of 'the crowds, the Roman soldiers, and the man
Jesus carrying his cross.' Just then our eighty-two-
year-old janitor passed slowly along the porch outside
the window, and peered in at the women in Eastern
costumes who were peering out, he thought, at him.
He was completely mystified at what was going on. The
illusion was shattered, of course, and we laughingly
threatened him that if he passed the window on the afternoon of the performance, he must at least be provided
with a spear and a Roman helmet. The day of the performance came, and I realised the success of the production,
when, at the end of the play, there was absolute silence
for a moment, and some of the audience had tears in their

eyes. I like to think they were overcome by the poignancy of the play.

After that we attempted other plays. One, a play about Florence Nightingale, needed a Victorian setting. With the aid of two large screens, heavy red velvet drapes, and a few pieces of Victorian furniture and bric-a-brac, we achieved a delightfully authentic setting. There was even a cleverly contrived garden entrance with massed Spring flowers (plastic of course, but realistic enough from a distance), and the whole thing was amazingly effective. Another play about the Court of Henry VIII we were to perform at the home of a church member. One of our group went to the beautiful house, which stood on the bank of the Penobscot River, to see what facilities we might be able to use to create a scene in a palace. She returned in great triumph. Apparently the dining area of our hostess's home was raised, with stairs leading to a large lounge below. This was perfect. 'Anne Boleyn' had persuaded our hostess to remove all her dining room furniture, to raise her beautiful crystal chandelier so that we would not knock our heads on it, and to drape heavy red velvet against the back wall, and on the 'throne' (one of her dining chairs). With the superb crystal sconces behind the 'throne' and the chandelier above, it really was 'palatial.' Some of our gorgeous costumes came from the most unlikely places. The local Thrift Shop was the source of some of our best 'finds'. We managed to obtain some really splendid velvet gowns, brocade tunics, and silken cloaks. Some of the superb costume jewellery came from rummage sales, and a gold and pearl coronet (fake, of course) and some sparkling buckles and clips, came from, of all places, the town dump. A clothing factory had discarded it, and one of the members of the cast had salvaged it. The end result was highly effective, and we certainly had a lot of fun.

But the Winter months pass slowly. One day as I

trudged with difficulty along the icy road to the store, the cheerful voice of a neighbour hailed me. 'Hi! I haven't seen much of you lately. Cabin fever?' I wasn't quite sure what she meant, but a few days later, an article in the *Bangor Daily News* intrigued me. It was headed 'Suffering from cabin fever? Go talk to the birds.' It was written by a Nathan Greenburg, Professor at the Abraham Lincoln School of Medicine at the University of Illinois. He had made a study of 'cabin fever' which is so well known in areas where the Winters are long and restricting, such as Norway. Professor Greenburg wrote, 'Got cabin fever? Get out and talk to the trees, the birds, and the snow. In Norway during the long Winter months people have been talking to the trees for centuries. Fantasize a little. Create a companion around you. You don't have to stay inside and just talk to plants. Get out and talk to birds, trees and snow — create something to relate to.' He warned, 'You will have to be strong-minded to do it. You mustn't be embarrassed if someone catches you saying something sweet to a tree. It may seem a frivolous thing to change something about yourself like a hairstyle, but it can have a profound effect on your self-image when you have the blahs.' Professor Greenburg wrote that it was not uncommon during a severe and relentless winter for families to succumb to a state of regression. 'They revert to the young child stage in which they feel powerless to change their environment. They feel isolated and cut off from their regular stimuli, and are forced into relationships with family members that are fraught with conflicts that can erupt into quarrels, leading to violent behaviour. Cases of wife beatings and child abuse generally increase. The public needs to understand that it is normal to feel frustrated because of the long hard Winter. Medical education may help combat potential severe depressions and perhaps even possible suicides.' He wrote, 'The main thing is to learn how to cope with the Winter. Coping depends how well a person deals with the constriction and restriction.'

I began to realise how real a problem 'cabin fever' is in Maine when I read in the *Bangor Daily News* of the dramatic increase in the State of child abuse and wife beatings. The Eastern Maine Medical Centre advertised lectures by doctors on how to combat this 'cabin fever' and invited the public to attend. I felt that going out talking to trees and snow and birds (if I could find any) was not going to be very constructive or productive. I decided, instead, to find out all about this State in which I lived, its early days, and some of the people who had helped to shape its history.

On the surface, there appeared at first nothing significant historically about Maine. However, as I read and delved more and more, I became fascinated by some of the colourful, dynamic, and intensely interesting characters who had lived in Maine in its early days, and whose lives had left an indelible mark on this unique State. There was the French Jesuit priest who, in the seventeenth century, lived among the Indians as a missionary for over thirty years. There were the huge, rough, tough lumbermen and river drivers, who contributed by their brawn and tenacity to Maine's early prosperity, and who made their annual descent on the town of Bangor, and 'painted it red.' There were the early settlers and their courage in face of great danger and hardships. There were, too, the Penobscot Indians, their culture and customs, and some of their unforgettable chieftains, one of whom gave his name to the town in which I lived. The actual founder of Maine, Sir Ferdinando Gorges, spent his life, or a great part of it, as Commander of the Plymouth Fort in Plymouth, England, which is my own home town.

Before long I was deeply immersed in finding out all I could about these people and their lives. This project certainly proved a real antidote to 'cabin fever', and extremely satisfying.

Just as it seems that Winter will never end, the first faint hints of Spring appear, with bird songs, a change in the wind. One waits and waits, looking each morning for a sign, the first green spear of the crocus, a subtle warmth in the air. Usually by the end of April there is the fragrance of damp earth freed at last from its blanket of snow, and the streams and rivers start to flow again. At the end of April there are canoe races on the Kenduskeag River, in which several of our church members participate. It is thrilling to watch the slim, graceful canoes plunge and glide through the spray of the fast-flowing icy water. Many capsize as they try to manoeuvre their canoes through the rapids, but men are stationed at strategic places in order to rescue them immediately. In May the lilacs burst into full beauty, and it is time for the gardens to be planted with beans, corn, beets, squashes, tomatoes and pumpkins. A bit of the pioneer spirit seems to still exist in the way Maine people till and rake and plant their gardens so fervently and methodically each Spring, thus ensuring a later abundant harvest. In May the church holds a Green Thumb Sale at which all kinds of plants are sold. We buy some, and plant a box in the Parsonage with scarlet geraniums, and pink and purple petunias, which are guaranteed to bloom all through the long hot Summer. Soon the vivid orange lilies which seem to grow wild everywhere, are there, a blaze of colour at the side of the road leading from the top of the hill to the Parsonage. The phoebes begin to nest in the eaves of the Parsonage porch again, with tremendous activity and enthusiasm, and all too soon, it seems, the first black fly makes its insidious appearance, and we know Summer has arrived at last.

Chapter 2

The People of the Dawn.

A few miles from my home in Orono is the town of Old Town. Although the name of this town is English, its connotation is Indian. It is the site of the 'old town' of Maine's earliest inhabitants, known as the Red Paint people because of their custom of placing in the graves of their dead, clay stained red with iron oxide. Many of these old cemeteries have been found in New England, especially in Maine. One of these was found at Old Town. In some of the old cemeteries in Maine there are indications that communal burials took place, probably in the Spring, when bodies of those who had died in the Winter were buried in a single large excavation, the floor of which was strewn with a layer of red ochre. Several hundred graves have been opened by the Peabody Museum of Cambridge, Massachusetts, and by the Department of Archaeology of Phillips Academy at Andover. The graves are so old that in nearly every instance the skeleton had completely disintegrated, or only a few small fragments were found in two of three. Thousands of stone implements have been unearthed, too, during the explorations: adze blades, fire-making sets, chipped flint knives, long, slender lance heads and projectile points, sharpening stones, and other types of implements. In one of the graves a beautiful quartz ball was found, which had been pecked into shape and polished. Some of the articles bore traces of red paint which came off in fine flakes when exposed to the air.

Certain phases of the culture of the ancient people who existed in what is now New England may be noted among the Eskimo and the now extinct Beothuk of Newfoundland. The Beothuk, too, painted their bodies and almost all of their possessions with this pigment of red ochre which they called 'odmet'. In fact the term Red Indian was given to them by the early navigators who visited Newfoundland, because of this custom. They were physically very much like their Algonquian neighbours, they wore similar clothing, similar tools were used by them, and their Summer homes were identical. In his book *The Beothuks or Red Indians* (Cambridge University Press, 1915) J. P. Howley wrote, 'It appears to have been their universal practice to smear everything they possessed with this pigment. Not only their clothing, but implements, ornaments, canoes, bows and arrows, drinking cups, even their own bodies were so treated. Small packages of this material tied up in birch bark are found buried with their dead.'

From 1669, Indian Island at Old Town seems to have been the principal settlement of the Penobscot tribe of Indians. In old French maps and documents it was known as Panouamske, and in English sources as Pannawambs-kek. The reservation of the Penobscot Indians is only three miles in length, and a mile and a quarter at the widest point. The island lies in the Penobscot River, and until a bridge was built in 1950, the only means of crossing the river was by boat, and by sled in Winter.

From childhood I had always been fascinated by the proud, aquiline features of the Indians, and as soon as I discovered there was an Indian reservation so close to Orono I couldn't wait to visit it. In my mind's eye I could see the conical tepees, the Indians in their deer-skin tunics and leggings, the papooses strapped to their mothers' backs. It was a clear, late Fall day when we made our first visit to the island. Reaching Old Town, a rather nondescript, dejected sort of town, we crossed the bridge, passing a colourful, painted sign denoting that this was the home of the Penobscot Indians. My anticipation mounted with every yard we progressed. We passed a white, wooden Catholic church, then a small school, then a graveyard, and then some small, down-at-heel wooden houses, some with derelict cars rotting outside. A group of rather swarthy-skinned youths with raven black hair, dressed in ordinary clothing, passed by unsmilingly, and a rather mangy dog barked at our car. Could this be it? How foolish and naive of me to suppose that life would stand still for the Indians. I felt a sense of disappointment that yet another of my illusions had been shattered, and that something colourful and real had been lost forever.

As the older Indians die, it seems, unfortunately, that the Indian crafts are dying with them, and are not being carried on by the younger generation. I wanted to buy an example of the Penobscot Indians' crafts before it was too late. I already had one of their delightful sweet grass baskets. Now I wanted a piece of their wood carving, and was told there was only one remaining Indian who did this work on the island. One cold January day I persuaded a friend to come with me, and we set off to find the house where such carvings were for sale. At last we found the place. Two small, black haired, sloe-eyed children stood outside. They stared unsmilingly as we approached. 'Is your mother in?' I asked. There was no reply, no change of expression, so I walked up the rickety steps leading to the house and knocked at the door. Again no reply. As there was a glass panel in the door, I peered through, and saw, reclining on a settee, a huge figure of a man. He stared back at me and made no attempt to rise, so I boldly opened the door, and said, 'I was told you have some carved sticks. I wish to buy one.' The Indian looked stolidly at me, then jerked his thumb toward

another room, grunting something unintelligible. A dark
haired, sallow skinned girl moved silently toward me, and
I repeated my request. She led me to a small room,
piled with baskets made from the sweet grass, some of
which hung in hanks on the walls. There was some attractive bead work, a huge tom-tom, and some sticks
carved with Indian symbols, and Indian heads or snakes'
heads. I chose a black painted stick with white symbols,
and a carved brave's head, uncoloured, but varnished.
Then I saw the war-club. Carved, as apparently all war-
clubs were, from a knot of wood, it had a proud, life-like
Indian's face, and on either side of the head were two
sharply carved points. The handle was carved with
symbols of tepees with smoke arising from the fire, a
turtle, and arrows. I could see that the war-club must
have been a formidable weapon. It was far too expensive,
unfortunately, so I had to be content with the cheaper
stick, but left, resolved to return when I had saved sufficient for this magnificent piece of work. As we were
leaving, several Indians entered the house, wearing red
and black checked woollen jackets, their long hair, black
and gleaming, caught back in a kind of pony-tail, and all
silent and uncommunicative.

Later I was able to purchase my war-club, and consider
it one of my most prized possessions. It was carved by an
Indian by the name of Senabeh, who was found dead in
his cabin a few months later. Senabeh Francis was not
only an accomplished wood-carver. He was a medicine
man of the Penobscot Indians. His people called him
'Senabeh — first man, creature of the Great Spirit.' His
father was a travelling musician, and Senabeh was born
in 1913, practically in a canoe on the Penobscot River.

When he was a child, Senabeh spent a great deal of
time with the elders of the tribe. At an early age he found
he had a gift of healing with herbs, a gift passed on to him
by his mother, and encouraged by her. At the age of
twenty, he went to live on an uninhabited island, twelve

miles from the Penobscot reservation. This was known as
Hemlock Island, and it was there Senabeh spent the
next twenty six years of his life. He called his island
Shangri-la, his paradise. Everything he needed in life was
there. It was his drug-store, where he obtained all his
medicines, his lumber yard, where he obtained all his
materials for carving, as well as his food supply. There
were rabbits, partridges, deer, ducks and moose. In the
Winter he would ice-fish, and in the Summer he would
eat organic foods, such as greens and fiddle-heads.
Senabeh grew herbs as well as vegetables on his island.
These he gathered and dried for his people. Every two
or three weeks Senabeh travelled twelve miles by canoe to
the reservation, taking with him some of his carvings and
herbal cures. After getting a fresh supply of provisions,
he would then travel back to his island retreat the same
day.

In 1979, not long before he died, Senabeh was inter-
viewed for the New England magazine, *Salt*. In it, he
said, 'A medicine man has to be spiritually inclined.
Medicine men are born, not made. He has to inherit
that spiritual power. His forefathers were spiritual.
Therefore, in each generation, it appears in a family.
Before a man may become a medicine man, he must go
up into the mountains to meditate. It is an essential
preparation. A medicine man is usually the second
leader of his tribe. His task is to advise his people, and
to keep them healthy.'

Senabeh was something of a mystic. He would sit for
hours in the dark, meditating, so that he could more
readily help his people to make wise decisions. He felt
that by living as he did, close to nature, he would become
a better man, and that way would live a cleaner way,
with cleaner thoughts.

Senabeh said the Indian gave thanks for everything
around him, the trees, the air he breathed, the water,
the fire, and the powerful things of the universe. 'We

don't pray from a book,' he said, 'we pray just the way we feel. We soul search.' Senabeh cared nothing for material things. He felt his wealth was all around him in the woods.

It was World War II that took Senabeh from his island. His conscience demanded that he join his tribal brothers to fight in the war in Europe from 1941 to 1945.

On his return, Senabeh could not reconcile the violence of those years with the spiritual life he had practiced for so long in the woods. He could never regain his former peace with himself and his surroundings ever again. It was then he began to drift and to drink. He became an itinerant craftsman going from one craft shop to another, being given room and board in return for making Indian artifacts.

Eventually, Senabeh settled back on Indian Island, first in a hut he had built, and then in a trailer, a gift from his people for his old age.

A steady pilgrimage of young Indians from the Passamaquoddy, the Micmac, and the Malecite tribes, as well as those from his own Penobscot tribe, visited Senabeh, bringing him gifts, and asking advice from this man with the gentle, yet troubled eyes.

This, then, was Senabeh, the Indian who had carved my war-club — a man whom I unfortunately had never met. Yet perhaps a little of his spirit remains in the wood he carved so well. I hope so.

I have become completely absorbed and fascinated with the history, the customs and colourful past of the Penobscot Indians, and I hope to weave all my gathered facts into a comprehensive picture, which will convey to my grandchildren in England something of the inventiveness and inherent kindness of this now sadly depleted race.

Within historic times the New England Indians have all been of the great Algonquian stock, and when the first settlers arrived in Maine they found it inhabited by many tribes of Indians. Most of these were part of the powerful Abenaki (or Wabenaki) nation. Waban meant dawn, and aki meant land in the Indian language, so the people were known as 'Dawnlanders' or 'The people of the dawn.' Each of the tribes had its own customs, its own chiefs, and its own types of canoe and houses. They could all speak easily with one another, although with different dialects. At that time the Indians were almost entirely confined to the coastal areas and the banks of the rivers. (The vast forest wilderness of the interior was inhabited mainly by wild animals.) At the present time only two of these tribes remain. They are the Pestumokadyik or 'spearers of pollock' now known as the Passamaquod-dies, and the Penobscot tribe. Many years of bloody warfare between white man and Indian, and with other tribes such as the savage Mohawks, as well as death from the diseases and epidemics, such as smallpox, introduced by settlers from Europe, have taken their toll.

The Indians used the resources of Nature intelligently to provide them with clothing, food and shelter. The forests abounded in vast numbers of deer, moose, bear and other animals, and the Indians hunted these with their bows and arrows, or trapped them in snares. The deer supplied them not only with meat, but also with clothing. Ducks, geese, and great droves of wild turkeys flocked everywhere, and the Indians found them easy prey and excellent eating. There were wild fruits of all kinds in great abundance, grapes, plums, strawberries, blueberries, cranberries, raspberries, blackberries, nuts and edible roots. These were gathered, spread out to dry, and packed in baskets for Winter use. They could be eaten dried, or soaked in water and eaten with maple syrup (which they obtained from the maple tree) or added to stews. The ocherous earths and the juices of plants and trees provided brilliant pigments and dyes. The materials were gathered, put into a vessel over the fire, covered with water and boiled until the liquid became coloured. A rich olive green was obtained from cedar leaves and bark, various berries and alder bark gave a dark red, rotten wood gave a dark blue, and white maple gave a light blue. Ash bark and its ashes gave yellow, and pine or hemlock bark gave a dark reddish brown.

The Indians had well cultivated gardens in which they grew corn, beans, pumpkins, squashes and tobacco. Each family had one or more gardens, sometimes a mile or more apart. They were meticulous in weeding, pruning, and fertilizing, and were said to have exceeded the English settlers in the care of their fields. The corn was harvested by the women and dried on mats. It was then stored in caches, in baskets, and in wooden receptacles made by cutting hollow logs into sections. Their barns were holes made in the earth. There are many legends of how men first received the corn seeds. One of these said that the seeds had been given to two hunters by a beautiful woman with whom the hunters had shared their last bit of food. The woman had long, light hair, and it was said that when the cornsilk (her hair) appeared, the corn was ready. The Indians never forgot to give thanks to the 'Great Spirit' for the gift of corn.

The food of the Indians varied according to the season. In the Spring they stayed by the rivers to catch the alewives, shad, salmon and sturgeon. The fish came up the rivers in huge shoals, and at the foot of every fall, men, women and children scooped up the fish in baskets, or caught them in rough weirs. Salmon was speared as it came upstream, or with hook and line or nets. Then came the planting of their crops of beans, corn and squash. After planting their gardens, the people within reasonable access to the coast went there to catch seal and porpoise for their oil and skins, as well as for food. They caught quantities of lobsters, dug clams and oysters, and dried them by smoking them, packing them in birch bark boxes for Winter consumption. From the sea birds they got feathers, which they used for decorative purposes. They returned home to harvest their crops, gathered berries, roots of all kinds, and nuts. Acorns were gathered, shelled, and ground into meal, which was used for thickening stews. The bitter principle in the acorn was removed by boiling in lye made from rotten maplewood ashes. The roots of the ground nut and yellow meadow lily were dug. Hulled corn and hominy were primitive Indian dishes, succotash was a mixture of corn and beans boiled, and a staple dish was a stew of corn or corn meal, beans, fish or meat (either dried or fresh), pumpkins, squashes and various roots. Various preparations were made from maize. Nokake, one of the most used, consisted of kernels parched in hot ashes and ground. Corn meal dough sometimes mixed with dried berries was made into little cakes, wrapped in leaves, and baked in hot ashes.

Soon after the harvest came the hunting season. The Indians were naturally expert hunters and trappers. Deer were trapped in snares attached to a spring pole baited with acorns or were taken in organized drives. V shaped fences were built a mile or two in length. During the day hunters would wait near the opening where the two sides converged and shoot the deer as they passed through. Snares were also set at the opening during the night. In October they moved deeper into the woods and prepared their traps for the Fall fur hunt, and after several weeks of feasting in their village returned once again to the forest to trap and hunt for moose.

During the Winter months the Indians lived on their stores of beans, acorns, nuts, dried berries, dried meat and fish and clams, and upon whatever fresh meat they were able to procure. All through the Winter they worked upon garments, weapons and ornaments. They made baskets from the sweet smelling sweet grass, and wampum from conch and quahog shells. As soon as the ice broke up they made their Spring catch of otter, beaver and muskrat, and soon were ready once again for fishing and the planting of their crops. Muskrat hunting was very important. They were hunted and trapped in the Spring and Fall. Every part of the flesh was eaten with great relish by the Indians and the pelts were sold.

Food was preserved for the Winter by smoking the meat and fish. This was done by laying the fish or meat on horizontal poles laid on two upright crotches with a slow burning fire beneath. Moose and deer meat were the meat staples for a great part of the year, and whatever was not eaten fresh was cut into strips several inches thick and smoked until it was dried like leather. This meat could be kept indefinitely and could be stewed or eaten just as it was. A concentrated food consisting of lean meat dried, pounded fine and mixed with melted fat was used a great deal by the Indians. This was known as pemmican. Butter was made from bear's fat. Dried clams and oysters were boiled in water, seasoned with ground acorns to give it flavour, and with bear or seal oil added made a tasty meal. This might be served in a great turtle shell or wooden bowl.

Clothing and tepees were made from the hides of animals. The skins were first scraped clean with a sharp edged stone, they were then rubbed briskly for a long time with smooth stones, which squeezed the oil from the hides, leaving them smooth, soft and supple. They were then ready to be made into dresses, tunics, leggings, moccasins and tepee coverings. Warm and serviceable clothing was made, too, from moose hair, the fibre of the milk weed and other materials. The women worked on the skins with thread made from the sinews of animals, using an awl or a needle made from a bone from the sable. This had an eye like the eye of a needle, and was ready for use after the other end of the bone was sharpened to a point. The awl was often the sharp tail of the horse-shoe crab or sea turtle.

The birch bark (mus-queh) was of immense importance to the Maine Indian. In fact it would have been difficult for him to have survived without it. The covering of his tepee, the roof of his permanent home, and utensils such as boxes, buckets, kettles, bowls and pots were made from it. Toboggans of thin wood and birch bark hauled their burdens across the snow. A sheet of birch bark could be a mat to sit on, a table covering, or a cover from the rain. The inner bark was a beautiful dark brown, and was easily ornamented by scraping upon it a pattern which showed up light against the dark background. The Penobscot designs were clever and artistic. This fine inner bark, carefully rolled and inscribed with strange symbols, recorded their treaties. The Indians used the roots of the spruce tree for all coarser work. The white spruce roots were best, and the women were responsible for digging the roots from soft soil. They dug until they found a good root about an inch in diameter near the butt end. They worked it out of the ground while it was still attached to the tree, then cut it off, trimmed it, thinned it down to the required size, then wound it in a coil in pieces from three to five feet long. Utensils were sewn with good spruce roots and then sealed with spruce gum. A birch bark pot, if kept full of water and placed over a slow burning fire could be treated almost like an iron kettle. The most permanent birch bark utensils were made from the heavy Winter bark. This was harder to remove, but more durable, and when this was stripped, cut into the desired shape, and sewn with spruce roots, made superior water-tight vessels.

The usual Summer dwelling of the Penobscots was the conical birch bark wigwam (wi 'gwom, camp or habita-tion) or tepee. These were usually about eight to ten

feet in height inside, and about ten feet in diameter at
the base. A framework of poles supported the bark
covering. Sheets of heavy birch bark about three and a
half feet wide were sewn together with spruce roots and
stretched over the poles. Another series of poles or
lengths of wood was placed outside to hold it in position.
An opening between the top edge of the covering and the
intersection of poles was the smoke hole. The indoor
fire-place in the wigwam was dug below the surface of
the floor. The cooking pots hung over it, suspended by a
hook from a pole which went from one side of the wigwam
to the other. The door flap was a tanned moose hide
laced to a pole at the upper and lower end. Woven bulrush
mats were used for lining the interior of the wigwam,
for covering, for sitting or lying on, for drying shelled
corn, berries, and innumerable other purposes. They
were used, too, for wrapping the body of a dead person,
or to serve as a protection for the various personal belongings buried with him.

A square or rectangular wigwam was erected for
better protection in the Winter. The lower part consisted
of four or five tiers of logs built up in the usual log cabin
style, while the upper part was a roof of birch bark
supported by poles. The crevices between the logs were
tightly packed with moss in order to keep out the cold
winds, and for further protection the walls were banked
with moss, earth and leaves. In the really cold weather
fir boughs were stacked against the outside. Inside the
wigwam platforms on each side, or layers of boughs on
the ground were placed for sitting or sleeping. Men,
women and children sat cross-legged, ate with their
fingers, and slept with perhaps a bearskin underneath
for warmth and a few blankets over them. There was no
other furniture.

The birch bark canoe (ar-quee-dun) was the master-
piece of the Indian. The Penobscot canoe was usually
about eighteen feet long. Birch bark was used for the

outer covering, with white cedar for the ribs, the rails and lining. Spruce roots were used for sewing, and pitch for the seams. The best canoe barks were those peeled in Winter, before the sap rises in the tree, when the bark is thick and tough as leather. A small fire was built near enough to loosen the bark, and then it was carefully peeled off. When the bark was removed in a single sheet it was rolled up, making a bundle from five to six feet long. A roll of bark could be kept indefinitely and soaked when wanted. In this way a canoe could be built in Summer out of the tougher Winter bark. There was seldom any ornamentation on the canoes except for the 'eyes' at the bow, and occasionally some etching. The 'eyes' were often a small circle or star placed on each side of the canoe at one end. The Indians believed they enabled the canoe to see any rocks and dangers ahead. The canoe had to be light, yet strong and resilient enough to withstand the rapids of swift and rocky rivers. These birch bark canoes are famous for their design, and the Old Town Canoe Company, one of the nation's leading manufacturers of canoes, still uses their pattern. Visitors to the factory are able to watch the process of canoe construction, from steaming and binding the bows to the varnishing of the finished product. To glide over the surface of one of the Maine lakes in a light and graceful canoe is an experience never to be forgotten. One is reminded of Longfellow's romantic lines from *Hiawatha*:

> I a light canoe will build me
> That will float upon the water,
> Like a yellow leaf in Autumn,
> Like a yellow water-lily.

John S. Springer, who had spent many years in active participation in the life of the forests described the Indian canoe in his book *Forest Life and Forest Trees* (New York, 1851). He wrote that the canoe was 'as a conveyance which seems to occupy a space between riding and flying,' and that 'its fairy-like buoyancy quite dissipates the idea of one's gravity.'

Heavy snows cover the ground for sometimes five months or more in Winter in Maine, and the Indians constructed the snow-shoe to enable them to walk on the deep snow. This was constructed of light ash ribs for the frame, and with an intricate pattern of moose hide webbing, woven closely whilst it was wet, so that it never sagged. The men cut the hide and made the frames, and the women usually did the webbing.

The Penobscot Indians excelled at basket making, and today this is their main surviving craft. The wood they used was the young black ash, which the Indians called brown ash. Basket stuff was manufactured by pounding the logs, which were from eight to twelve feet long and from five to ten inches in diameter, with the side of an axe head, until the bruised wood separated into layers. It took about two to three hours of hard work to finish a log. Today a machine does the beating of the log and accomplishes in half an hour more than a man with an axe could do in three hours. The sweet grass basket is still being made today on Indian Island. Older people of Maine vividly remember the visits of Indian basket-makers over half a century ago, when as children they watched with excitement when Indian women made the rounds of village houses in the Spring. Baskets of every shape and size were strapped to the Indian's back, and hung in such profusion from her arms, shoulders and waist that she could hardly be seen. There were baskets for laundry, sewing, for men's starched collars, and miniature baskets for children. In spite of the dwindling supply of ash and sweet grass, the Indians still follow this ancient craft of their people and most of them adhere to the traditional designs.

Before the time when the French and English settled in Maine, and cloth could be obtained in trade, clothing was made entirely from the skin or hair of animals. Old pieces of Indian dress, preserved in museums and among the Indians themselves, serve to remind us of their original style of dress. The men wore moccasins, leggings (often ornamented with designs in red, blue and yellow), a breech cloth, and the typically North Eastern long sleeved coat. This long coat reached half way to the knee, and was open down the front with one thong fastening. These garments were made from moose, deer, or caribou skins, with ornamentation on the collar, shoulder seams, around the cuffs, the front opening, and around the lower edge. The design was often diamond shaped, or with flower and plant symbols. An invariable part of a man's costume was his 'pitsonungan' or wallet. This was the skin of a mink, sable, or woodchuck. Tanning made it pliable and preserved it. When slipped under the belt it formed a bag in which the pipe, tobacco, flint and other possessions could be carried. Later, when the Indians traded with the settlers, their leggings were usually of red or blue cloth. In the Winter the leggings were fastened inside the moccasins, which were usually made of moose skin. The cloth leggings had a flap several inches wide, and this was often decorated with bead work or ribbon applique. The leather ones had a fringe along the seam. Leggings were also made of muskrat skins, which were usually plain and fringeless. The breech cloth was made from tanned skin and was supported by a girdle from which the ends hung in front and behind. In Summer this was frequently the only garment worn. Robes or coats for cold weather were made from the skins of the bear, moose, deer, wolf, beaver, otter, fox, raccoon and squirrel. A robe of raccoon skins was particularly valued because of the tails which would ornament the garment. Sometimes the men wore caps for hunting. These had two ears which were intended as decoys. A cape at the back would keep off the snow.

On ceremonial occasions the men wore quite elaborate costumes. Rosettes of feathers were attached to their arms, and the belts and garments were fringed with feathers and colourful with porcupine quills, moose hair, or wampum decoration. Turkey and eagle feathers were worn by the men. These were worn on a head band and fashioned like a coronet, with the feathers standing stiffly upright, broadwise like a fan or a turkey cock's train. Sometimes a beaded head-band with partridge wings on either side, or a partridge tail in front or behind was worn. The feathers of the gull, the blue heron and the hawk were also used. The most typical ornamental head dress for braves and squaws, however, was a decorated band with a circlet of feathers, or a single, large upright feather at the back.

The skirt was of major importance in the women's clothing. This consisted of a length of skin (later of cloth) which reached from the waist to the middle of the lower part of the leg. Bead and ribbon work ornamented the seam, and it was secured by a cord. Beneath it leggings were worn, and these, too, had decorated outer flaps. The women's upper garment was sometimes of weasel or hare skins sewn together. Later they were made of bright coloured calico material. The women sometimes wore long, peaked, hood-like caps, colourful with bead and ribbon work. As a protection against heavy rain the Indians stripped off a large piece of bark, cut a hole in the centre for the head to go through, and let the ends hang down over the shoulders. This was supplemented by a conical birch bark hat made by sewing with spruce roots, or pinning with a piece of bone the edge of a flat cone to fit the head.

The Penobscots wore moccasins of deer and moose skin. Inside the home a loose slipper was worn, and a low, heavy shoe or oiled moose moccasin was worn in the woods. These were sewn with a stout thong. The entire moose hock served as a boot for Winter wear. These were warm and waterproof, and exceptionally useful in the snow and in the Spring thaws. Several layers of warm stockings of hare skin were worn when the weather was cold, and, later, moose wool stockings. Both men and women wore mittens of fur and heavy fur robes.

The men, particularly the hunters, wore necklaces of deer antler prongs, and deer hooves, bored and strung on leather thongs. Necklaces of bears' claws indicated high rank, and were considered a protective charm if the wearer had killed the bear himself. The women loved to wear bright colours and beads. For ceremonial and other important occasions the men, and sometimes the women, painted their faces. The paint was obtained from vari-coloured clay streaks, and was kept in a pot to preserve its potency and colour. Until long after the arrival of the settlers, the Abenaki men shaved their heads except for a scalp lock tied close to the crown. Combs were made of wood, and were about two and a half to three inches across, with deeply notched teeth. The dried skin of a porcupine's tail was used as a hairbrush or a comb cleaner. A wooden back scratcher was a piece of thin ash, fourteen to twenty four inches long, with a notched and curved bend an inch or so wide. Often the older women sat in the evenings scratching away under their clothing, and grunting contentedly.

Dancing was one of the principal amusements of the Indians, and in the Summer both men and women loved to bathe in the lakes and rivers. Apparently the men had a type of sauna or sweat lodge. This was a little circular cell or cave made on the side of a hill near a rivulet or brook. A fire was built in the centre over a heap of stones. The stones retained a great heat after the fire diminished, and around them a group of about twenty men would sit unclothed, for an hour or more, smoking their pipes, talking. They would then emerge and would run into the brook to cool themselves. In Winter they would probably roll in the snow. Smoking tobacco was another habitual amusement enjoyed by both sexes, and at friendly gatherings the lighted pipe was passed from one to the other, each taking a few puffs. The calumet, or peace pipe, had a bowl usually of soft reddish stone, and a stem of the hardest wood. It was usually about two feet in length, and often ornamented. To smoke from this pipe was a seal or contract of mutual friendship and peace, and served as a sacred pledge of faith and honour.

The Indians discovered the healing properties of plants, herbs, barks, and roots, and cures for fevers and other ailments, and some of these the white men learned from them, as well as many other useful arts. The Indians found in the wild plants, shrubs and trees healing properties for almost every physical ailment to which they were vulnerable. They experimented and learned the virtues of each plant. In time this extensive knowledge of indigenous plants became the special property of the medicine men who ministered to the physical and spiritual needs of their people. However, herbal lore was common knowledge among most Indians, whether they were medicine men or not. For simple remedies not requiring the special skills of the medicine man, they could go out in the fields, collect the correct herb and prepare it themselves. As the early settlers who first encountered these so-called 'savages' using strange herbal brews were to learn, most of these herbal remedies seemed to work.

Even in the later Colonial era of America, the value of Indian methods was still appreciated. In 1798, Benjamin S. Barton, a botanist and member of the medical faculty at the University of Pennsylvania, addressed the Philadelphia Medical Society. To him it was 'obvious that the Indians of North America are in possession of a number of active and important remedies.' He continued, 'What treasures of medicine may not be expected from a people, who although destitute of the lights of science, have discovered some of the most inestimable medicines with which we are acquainted.' At one time or another almost two hundred drugs from indigenous plant sources that were used by the Indians were included in the United States Pharmacopoeia, the official source book of medicinal products.

The sensory awareness of the Indians was highly developed, and they had a special understanding of the natural environment. Their eyes, ears, and even their finger tips were sensitive and sure interpreters. They could travel the forest day or night with unerring footsteps, with only the stars as their compass, and could read from the bark of the trees what had passed that way. Their noses were as keen as foxes', and could scent danger at a distance, and they could tell by the leaves underfoot whether a stranger had entered their domain. In his book *Lame Deer, Seeker of Visions* (New York: Simon and Schuster, 1972), an Indian, John Fire (Lame Deer), described this special perceptiveness of the Indian:

> I'm an Indian. I think about ordinary, common things, like this old cooking pot. The bubbling water comes from the rain cloud. It represents the sky. The fire comes from the sun which warms all—men, animals, trees. The meat stands for the four-legged creatures, our animals, who gave of themselves so that we should live. The steam is living breath. It was water; now it goes up to the sky, becomes a cloud again. These things are sacred. Looking at the pot, full of good soup, I am thinking how, in this simple manner, the Great Spirit takes care of me. . . . We Indians live in a world of symbols and images where the spiritual and the commonplace are one. . . . These symbols are part of Nature, part of ourselves—the earth, the sun, the wind and the rain, stones, trees, animals, even little insects like ants and grasshoppers. We try to understand them, not with the head, but with the heart, and we need no more than a hint to give the meaning.

The Indians had their own unique methods of weather forecasting, too, which woodsmen today accept as indisputable forewarnings of weather changes. If smoke curled close to the ground, it meant rain that day. Loons crying at night were always calling for rain. If animals had heavy coats of fur in the Fall, it meant a Winter of deep snows. They judged their own preparations for

Winter by the amount of nuts the squirrels hoarded, and by the time the bears went into hibernation. In Winter if an owl hooted, or foxes barked on a ridge, this would mean a spell of warm weather coming during these colder months. A circle around the moon was a signal of stormy weather.

Maine Indian women, on the whole, were said to have been quite beautiful. As early as 1640 Sir John Jocelyn wrote of the Indian women whom he had observed at Black Point, in the vicinity of Portland: 'The women, many of them, have good features, all of them black eyed, having even, short teeth and very white; their hair black, thick and long; broad breasted; handsome, straight bodies and slender, considering their constant loose habit; their limbs cleanly straight and of a convenient stature; generally as plump as partridges, and, saving here and there one, of a modest deportment. Their garments are a pair of sleeves of deer or moose skin, dressed and drawn with lines of several colours into arabesque work, with buskins of the same; a short mantle of trading cloth, either blue or red, fastened with a knot under the chin, and girt about the middle with a zone wrought with white and blue beads into pretty works. Of these beads they have bracelets for their neck and arms, and links to hang in their ears, and a fair table curiously made up with beads likewise, to wear before their breasts. Their hair they comb backward, and tie it up short with a border about two handfuls broad, wrought in works as the other, with beads.'

As Indian mothers went about their daily tasks, the babies went along, too, carried in cradleboards on the mothers' backs. When gathering food or tending the crops in the fields, they hung the cradleboards, babies and all, on a nearby tree. The cradleboards were often beautifully carved and decorated with colourful pigments. When not in the cradleboard the Indian babies were kept in the baby hammock. This was made from either buckskin or a blanket. In fine weather the hammock was hung out of doors from trees, and at other times, indoors, suspended from tent poles or posts.

When lullabies or rocking failed to soothe a crying baby, its parents often gave it warm mint tea to drink, or if it were older, mint leaves to chew. Teething babies were given smooth bones to chew on. These were tied to the babies' wrists with strips of hide, so that they would not be swallowed. Nearly every young Indian child had a corn husk doll, and a typical food was made from corn mush with berries and maple syrup.

The Indians had no money except wampum. This was wrought from shells of the quahog or hard shell clam. The ends of the shells were polished and formed into cylindrical shaped beads. The principal part of the shell is white, but a portion of it, ranging from light purple through various shades to nearly black, was used for making the coloured beads, which had a commercial value double that of the white. The Indians regarded wampum as one of their most valuable possessions, and used it as currency, for recording treaties and for decorative ornaments. In 1648 Massachusetts ordered that wampum should be recognized as legal tender to the amount of forty shillings. In 1723 Father Sebastian Rasle, the French Jesuit priest, wrote of the value of wampum, from his mission at Norridgewock on the Kennebec River. 'It is with these beads that our Indians bind up and plait their hair on their ears and behind. They make of them pendants for their ears, collars, garters, large sashes, five or six inches in breadth, and on this kind of ornament they pride themselves much more than a European would on all his gold and silver.'

If an Indian wished to marry a squaw, he told his parents, who then talked to the bride's parents. If all went satisfactorily, the prospective husband sent the squaw a string of wampum, of sometimes one thousand beads, and presented her with wedding garments.

The families then met at the wigwam of the girl's parents, and the young couple sat together. They and the guests then feasted and danced, and then at last the married couple retired.

Some of the finest examples of wampum are to be found in the Peabody Museum of. Archaeology and Ethnology collections, Harvard University, Cambridge, Massachusetts. These were obtained from the Penobscot and other Maine Indians, by whom some of this beautiful woven wampum had been preserved through several generations.

When a death occurred in the village everything became very quiet, and any festivities which might have been taking place were immediately halted. The dead man was dressed in his best clothes, and his ornaments were placed on him. His bows and arrows (or later, his gun) were placed with him also. The body was wrapped in a roll of birch bark and buried several feet deep in the burial ground or 'grave habitation'. If someone died away from home, perhaps in distant hunting grounds, every effort was made to bring the body home for interment. Relatives and friends gathered and demonstrated their grief. Some elderly men standing near the corpse chanted a dirge and the others joined in. This is said to have been a prayer for the soul. In the *Bangor Daily Whig and Courier* of January 5th, 1835, there was a report of the discovery of such graves: 'A number of graves were found after a recent storm at Tiverton, Maine. In one grave were found seven gun barrels, two pistol barrels, six brass kettles, a large quantity of beads, several pieces of blanket, two clay pipes, iron pots, shoes, pieces of earthenware, pieces of the skins of animals, etc. They are, no doubt, the remains of a portion of the Indians who once inhabited this section of our country.'

At the head of every tribe was a Sachem, or supreme ruler. To be the chief of a tribe was a very responsible position, for upon the chief lay the task of feeding, protecting, and advising his people. Among New England tribes monogamy seems to have been the rule, although chiefs and men of wealth and distinction were allowed two or more wives. A Sachem was the absolute ruler of his people, and together with his councillors made major decisions regarding such matters as war and peace, the punishment of offenders, and so on. On important occasions all the principal men of the tribe were summoned to a large house which was built for council or ceremonial purposes. This was known as the long house, and here the chief and his advisors consulted. The old men spoke first, for they were venerated for their wisdom and experience. But it was upon the chief that the ultimate responsibility rested.

Joseph Orono was one of the most notable and well-loved chiefs of the Penobscot tribe of Indians. Most Maine historians have given the date of Orono's birth as 1688. The Penobscot tribe of which Orono was chief inhabited the country along the Penobscot River and the adjacent islands. Their principal villages were believed to be within the boundaries or in the immediate vicinity of the town of Orono. When the area later became settled, the white inhabitants grew to know him well and they respected and loved him for his fairness and kindly conduct. He was an outspoken advocate for peace between Indian and white men. William D. Williamson, in his *History of Maine* (1832), reported a talk that Orono had once given revealing his views on the subject. Some extracts of it are: 'Peace is the voice of the Great Spirit. Everyone is blessed under its wings. Everything withers in war. Indians are killed. Squaws starve. Nothing is gained — not plunder — not glory. Let the hatchet be buried. Smoke the calumet once more. Strive for peace.'

Joseph Orono was not a full-blooded Indian. He had blue eyes, a fair complexion, and hair of an auburn tinge, which became perfectly white in his old age. His heredity is still shrouded by hazy evidence. The early settlers believed that he had been captured by the Indians as a child, and adopted by the tribe. Orono himself said that his father was French and his mother half French and half Indian, but did not name his parents. General Henry Knox, who knew him well, wrote that Orono was 'half Indian, half French, of the Castine breed.' William D. Williamson, too, wrote that the chief was 'a reputed descendant of the Baron de Castin by an Indian wife.' The Baron was a French officer and adventurer, who headed a trading outpost at Pentagoet (now Castine) in the late 17th century. The Baron befriended the Indians and lived in much the same manner as they did. He married Chief Madockawando's daughter Mathilde, and was adopted into the tribe. Madockawando was a remarkable chief. His name meant 'wonder worker', and he was renowned as a great shaman.

Orono spoke both French and English besides his native tongue, but could neither read nor write. His mark or signature is debatable. Some historians have described it as a beaver, whilst others (in the *Centennial History of Orono, 1874*) call it a seal with a raised head. When the Revolutionary War began, Orono expressed his sympathy for his white neighbours, and offered the services of himself and his warriors to their cause. The Penobscots at this time were the most numerous, as well as the most powerful of the Maine Indians. Their warriors numbered about four hundred, and Orono said that if some of the grievances of his tribe were dealt with they would help the colonists wholeheartedly. He referred to the trespassing on the tribe's property, and some dishonesty in dealing with them. They were promised that these complaints would be investigated; consequently many of the tribe did eventually engage in the war. Orono died in February, 1801, at the reputed age of one hundred and thirteen years. An old resident of Orono, a Mrs. Hall, who had been present at Orono's funeral, recalled in 1874 that she remembered the chief as 'tall, straight and fine looking with blue eyes.' Orono was beloved by both white men and Indians, and was idolized by his tribe. Many tributes were paid to his memory, as well as the naming of a town in his honor. Mrs. Frances Mace, a native of Orono, wrote of him,

> Noblest among the braves was Orono,
> A kingly native, just and wise and true,
> Worthy of honour—well do we bestow
> On this his dwelling place the name of Orono.

Normally, it was customary for chiefs to be succeeded by male members of their own family, but Orono had had only two children. His son had been killed in a hunting accident as a young man, and his daughter had married a Captain Nicola, who had been a survivor at Norridgewock's massacre. There was no descendant whom the tribe wanted as the successor to their revered old chief, and quite a period of time elapsed before a new chief was appointed. In about 1806, the tribe chose Old Attean as their leader. Unfortunately, he lived only about three years after his appointment. He had travelled to Boston on tribal business, and becoming depressed and anxious over the business going wrong, had in desperation stabbed himself to death. Following Old Attean's death, the tribe chose Joe Nolan. He, too, died soon after his election as chief. Then in 1816, John Attean, the son of Old Attean, was elected Governor, with John Neptune as second chief, or Lieutenant Governor. Reliable documentary evidence shows that there were Neptunes among the Passamaquoddies, the Maliseets and Penobscots before 1760, and that they were an important family. They furnished many of the head chiefs and had been the signers of important documents. The inauguration of the two chiefs was held at Old Town in September, 1816, in the great wigwam, with delegates from the Malecite and Passamaquoddy tribes attending. Much inter-tribal visiting was carried on in the old days, when it was customary to assemble in order to inaugurate each others' chiefs.

The visiting party always arrived by canoe, flags flying from bow and stern. As soon as the visitors were sighted on the river, the people of the village gathered on the beach, the men in the foreground. The visitors halted their canoes in front of the assembled crowd, then in an even line the canoes were slowly paddled ashore, the occupants singing their special greeting song. Then the men of the village, armed with guns, formed two rows, and as the canoes approached, fired in salute. The chief of the visiting tribe landed from the foremost canoe, his men still chanting, and he, also chanting, walked between the rows of the hosts. The guns were fired again, then the flag in front of the chief's house was lowered and then raised again. The chiefs of the village then escorted the visiting chief to a special lodge, while the captains of the village carried the visitors' canoes from the water and set them before the guests' house. The flag was again lowered and raised, and then both groups mingled freely and informally. The rest of the day was spent in feasting and dancing, and visiting friends in the village.

The inauguration of John Attean and John Neptune was witnessed by the historian, William Durkee Williamson. He gives a long and detailed description of it in his *History of Maine* (1832). Fifteen or twenty delegates from each of the visiting tribes were present at the impressive installation ceremony, all attired in Indian fashion. Attean and Neptune wore coats of scarlet broadcloth, with brooches of silver and collars, arm-bands, and other ornaments of silver. Belts of wampum were brought into the great wigwam by the visiting chiefs, and these were presented to the chiefs being inducted to office, together with a lengthy speech. After the presentation of wampum, silver medals were hung about the necks of the new chiefs. The flag outside the building was raised and lowered as each was inducted. A priest then read from the Scriptures, and psalms and hymns were sung. A group of women then entered, wearing elaborately ornamented ceremonial dress, and performed a dance ceremony. An old woman carrying a walking cane led the file of dancers, who danced around the hall in a peculiar, shuffling fashion to the light beat of a drum. After completing the circuit they then retired. The ceremonies lasted for more than three hours, after which came the time of feasting and celebration. Two fat oxen had been killed and barbecued, and there were great dishes of rice, beans, vegetables and bread. The rest of the day was spent in sports and dancing, with games and contests of skill between the men of each tribe. The following days continued in revelry, until the visitors at length departed, their mission accomplished, and the village again resumed its normal life.

John Neptune was about forty nine years of age when he became Lieutenant Governor of the Penobscot tribe. According to Indian culture, he was well born, and had had ancestors in commanding positions. Neptune was a man of fine physique, and was a notable orator and a great hunter. Although he was not the titular head chief, it soon became apparent that John Neptune was in practice the real chief of the Penobscots. He was superior in intellect and personality to John Attean, and therefore gradually wielded more influence. He represented the tribe at important meetings, and expressed his views fluently and ably. When, in 1818, Massachusetts made a new treaty with the Penobscots, it was Neptune who replied to the Commissioners. Although he spoke in broken English, every word was distinct and easily understood, and his gestures were forceful. When he ably defended a member of his tribe who was accused of murdering a white man, the court-room listened spellbound, and Judge William Williamson recorded the speech as worthy of preservation. Williamson lived in

Bangor from 1806 to 1846. He had been postmaster, and Judge of Probate for Penobscot County before writing his *History of Maine* in 1832. Williamson knew both Neptune and Attean well. He described Attean as 'of a placid disposition, manifestly indicated by a bluish eye and a smiling countenance. In stature he is tall, straight, and well-proportioned; in intellect, in knowledge of business, and in ability to speak English, he holds a place inferior to several others. It is supposed he is not an unmixed native — perhaps a half-breed.' Of Neptune he wrote, 'Neptune is unquestionably a pristine, full-blooded Indian. He is of a copper colour; in person stout, thick-set, with broad shoulders, large face, high cheek bones, small mouth, and black sparkling eyes. His understanding, intelligence, and shrewdness are of the first order. He is very collected in his deportment, and always carries with him an air of authority. He is alto-gether superior to Attean in everything except character. For he is said to be the most lascivious Indian there ever was in the tribe. . . . The Indians say he is arbitrary and self-willed, makes too free with the ardent spirit (liquor) and has ten or a dozen bastard papooses. Hence his personal conduct and some of his official measures have occasioned him many foes, among whom are some of the likeliest Indians in the tribe.'

By 1816 the Penobscot tribe was sadly depleted in numbers, and its members poor and destitute. They, who had once been so numerous and powerful, and the sole possessors of the area, were now confined to limited reservations. A treaty had been ratified on October 11th, 1786, when the Indians had ceded more of their lands, and on June 24th, 1818, a meeting was held in Bangor between the chiefs of the Penobscot Indians and Commissioners from Massachusetts. The purpose of this meeting was to discuss the circumstances of the Indians, and to persuade them to relinquish more of their lands. Neptune and Attean were at this meeting.

The original document of the address to the Penobscots in Assembly at Bangor, 1818, was found among the papers of General John Blake and is now in the Special Collections of the library at the University of Maine. Blake had been the Government Agent to the Indians since 1811, and was to continue in this office until his resignation in 1821.

The address began:

Chiefs and Brothers of the Penobscot Tribe:

We acknowledge the goodness of Almighty God, the great and good Spirit, who hath made both you and us, and from whom all our blessings are received, that we are permitted to meet you here this day in peace and friendship, and as He is this year blessing the earth with the warmth of the sun, and the refreshing rain from the clouds, and giving us the prospect of a great abundance for the use of man and beast, it is the duty of both you and us to praise and adore Him with our whole hearts.

Brothers

We informed you by our letter which has been delivered you by General Blake, that we had been appointed by the General Court and your good father, our excellent Governor of this Commonwealth, to treat with you concerning the land and islands in your possession on Penobscot River, and also concerning the best means of improving your situation and condition in life; and we have also informed you that we should meet you here this day for that purpose.

Brothers

We have nothing in view, and shall make no proposals to you but such as will be for your benefit, and we desire that nothing should be done or agreed upon on your part, but by your own free will and consent.

Brothers

The General Court have impowered us to agree with you for the purchase of your right to the land and islands on Penobscot River which you now possess, and have a right to use for hunting and fishing. We thank you, therefore, to tell us plainly whether you are willing to sell us your right to these lands and islands. This is the first thing that we ask you to tell us; and we shall wait patiently for your answer before we make any particular proposals.

Brothers

If you tell us you are willing to sell your right to these lands and islands, we now declare to you that we are authorized to give and deliver you therefore, such articles as will feed and clothe you and your women and children, while you shall be hunting in the forest, and they shall be suffering in the cold and storms of Winter.

Brothers

We pray you to think well upon these things, and to give us a plain and ready answer, for we assure you that we mean to deal honestly with you and plainly. We should feel the vengeance of the Great Spirit who hates and punishes all falsehood and deception if we should attempt to deceive you. And we also assure you that the General Court and your good father, our excellent Governor, would highly disapprove our conduct and severely punish it, if we should attempt to do anything that was not for your good and that of the Commonwealth.

Brothers

If you should agree to sell us your rights to these lands and islands, and if we can agree on the terms thereof, we further declare to you that we are authorized and commanded by the General Court to examine into your situation and condition as men. The General Court consider you as their children, for they know you were made and protected and governed by the same kind parent and benefactor as ourselves. We will therefore propose and are ready to agree upon all proper means to improve your moral and religious habits and feelings . . . to learn you the use of tools for the improvement and tillage of the land. . . For it is the express command of the Great Spirit that we shall till the ground and subdue it. To afford you the means of obtaining useful knowledge for yourselves and your children. . . To persuade you to live industrious and useful lives. . . To abstain from the use of spiritous liquors which is the poison which has destroyed many white men and Indians, and caused them to melt away like snow before the fire. But above all things to persuade you to love and obey God and His son Jesus Christ, so that when you come to die, and leave the land to your children, and your mortal bodies be bound in its bosom, you may be prepared to live forever with your good friends and fathers that have gone before you.

Daniel Davis
Mark Langdon Hill   Bangor, June 24th, 1818.

A few days later a new treaty was signed by the Indians, whereby the Penobscots released all claims to their lands with the exception of the group of islands now occupied by them. In payment for this transfer, the Indians were to receive one six pound cannon, one swivel, fifty knives, two drums, four fifes, one box of pipes, three hundred yards of ribbon and two hundred yards of calico. From then onward, too, they were to receive annually

- 500 bushels of corn
- 15 barrels of wheat
- 7 barrels of clear pork
- 1 hogshead of molasses
- 100 yards of double width broadcloth, which was to be red one year and blue the next
- 50 good blankets
- 100 pounds of gunpowder
- 400 pounds of shot
- 6 boxes of chocolate
- 150 pounds of tobacco and 50 dollars in silver

Fannie Hardy Eckstorm, the Maine author, was an authority on the culture of the Penobscot Indians. In 1835, when Fannie's grandparents came to Brewer (which is across the river from Bangor, and about ten miles from Orono), more Indians than white people were living there. Apparently Brewer had been an ancient Indian resort. Fannie's grandfather kept a store there, and bought furs and articles made by the Indians. Her father had an Indian nursemaid when he was a child, and an Indian girl did the family's washing. As a boy, Fannie's father had played games with Indian boys in their wigwams and in the forest. Fannie, too, had Indian girl friends, and went to stay with one of them in her home on Indian Island.

An old Indian woman, who came selling baskets, and who carried with her a grimy pack of cards for telling fortunes, and a stubby black pipe in her bag, told Fannie tales of Indian magic and shamanism. The old woman said that m'teoulin were those who possessed many strange and wonderful powers. They knew things that white people did not know. They had fought with spirits, vanquished demons, and held the power of life and death over their enemies. She told Fannie strange stories of giants and dwarfs, fairies, elves, and talking animals, of magic and those who used it. In the Indian dialect 'mte' meant noise, 'ol' indicated something hollow, and 'ino' was Indian for person. So m'teoulin meant 'one who made a noise on something hollow.' It has been suggested that this was the origin of the tom-tom, the sound of which may have been originally designed to drive out evil spirits.

The power of shamanism was great among the Penobscot Indians, and they held in high regard the ability of selected individuals to control the unseen or spirit world. Among the Maine Indians, shamanism was commonly attributed to the greater chiefs, and the Neptune family, one of the noted lines of chiefs, was regarded as being particularly gifted 'meteoulinak' or magicians. Fannie Hardy Eckstorm wrote, 'It is among the Neptunes that we find the best genealogical material and the highest reputation for sorcery. Their magic power is still firmly believed in by many Indians, and it is from the Neptune family, if anywhere, that we must get our understanding of what our Indians used to regard the ability of selecting individuals to control the unseen world.' In his book *Penobscot Man* (1950), Dr. Frank Speck wrote, 'The Penobscot shaman seems to have been a wonder worker whose magic power was derived from the spiritual and animal world. He was a man who could meet the invisible forces upon their own ground, with magic.' John Neptune was said to have been one of the greatest shamans there ever was, and tales of his powers were told by many raconteurs. Neptune was far too shrewd to deny any wonderful feat attributed to him, and to discount any tales of wizardry credited to him. All added to his power and prestige.

As John Neptune's constant companion, Molly Molasses was a familiar figure around Bangor in the 1800's. Apparently she had never married, though Indian women told Fannie Hardy Eckstorm that Molly had had four children, and attributed them all to John Neptune. She was certainly Neptune's ally throughout his lifetime, and her loyalty to him was unfaltering always. Nobody seemed to know Molly's real name. The white people always called her by the name Molly Molasses. Some have thought her real name was Marie Pelagie Nicola. Others, the Indians particularly, said her name was Baylashee or Balassee, and that this had been distorted to Molasses. Molly was short, thick-set and 'chunky' but not fat. She had heavy features and a very dark complexion. She dressed in a short skirt and leggings, with a grey blanket over her shoulders and a pointed cap on her head. Her upper garment was a loose sacque. Up until the last years of her life she wore a necklace of wampum about two inches wide. In later life she wore a man's beaver hat encircled with a band of silver instead of the pointed cap normally worn by squaws. Molly is reputed to have had very keen, sharp eyes, and a very quick temper. It is said that on occasion she would swear fluently, and her face would become like a thunder cloud when anything angered her. One of her favourite expressions with which she prefaced enquiries was, 'What debble? What debble his name is?' Molly claimed to remember when the white people first came as settlers, and apparently told Fannie Hardy Eckstorm's grandfather, 'Couldn' understan' 'em; talk jus' like blackbirds.' Her friendship for Fannie's grandfather and father outweighed even family or tribal loyalty, and on many occasions she warned them of Indians who were stealing from them. Molly apparently had more influence with the tribe than anyone else except for Neptune, and she was highly respected by them. She was regarded as a witch by some, and an Indian told Fannie Hardy

Eckstorm, 'If she said you would die, you would die.' Even when she was old, lame and bent, Molly was able to dominate those around her. The *Bangor Daily Whig and Courier* of November 2nd, 1863, said of her a few years before her death, 'Molly Molasses, the grandmother of all the Penobscots, still frequents our streets, receiving kindly coppers from the third generation of those who have known her as an old woman. She has no fixed idea of her own age, but it must be considerably over a hundred. Though much bent, she walks with apparent strength.' Thoreau, too, wrote in *The Maine Woods* of a visit he made to the Allagash Lakes. On his way there, after leaving the steamer at Bangor, he and a companion passed Molly Molasses in the street. He wrote of her, 'As long as she lives the Penobscots may be considered extant as a tribe.'

It is thought that Molly died at Indian Island in January, 1868, aged about one hundred years. An article from *The Jeffersonian* of January 1868, may have been her obituary notice. It said of her, 'Molly was always "passed" free on board all the river steamers, received innumerable presents, all unsolicited, and was universally regarded with as much deference as if she was the benefactor, and not the beneficiary of all. It is hoped she had a free pass "over Jordan", for in this life no sin was ever attributed to her — except what was aboriginal.'

In addition to seven legitimate children, John Neptune had an unknown number of illegitimate offspring. One Indian informant said that Neptune "had been all lound (round) and got child most every place." When he was sixty years old, with a wife, children, and grandchildren, Neptune seduced the wife of his superior, John Attean. Seemingly forgetting his own honour and dignity, as well as that which he owed his tribe and his friend, Attean, Neptune committed this unpardonable sin in the absence of the husband. Attean first knew of his wife's unfaithfulness when the priest refused her absolution. Angrily demanding an explanation, Attean was told that his wife was expecting Neptune's child. In spite of his normally equable temperament, and perhaps already feeling inferior to Neptune, Attean was determined to wreak his revenge. Once he and Neptune were separated with great difficulty when they tried to kill each other in a combat with knives. The tribe was outraged and indignant at Neptune's behaviour. Until this time Neptune had escaped any serious consequences of his libertinism, but the tribe felt that this time he had gone too far, and Neptune was forced to flee from their anger. The first real split in the tribe came at the beginning of 1832, when Neptune gathered his family and sympathisers around him, and they all moved to Brewer, where they remained until 1850. For some years Neptune avoided his old hunting grounds, and kept well away from John Attean. Almost half the tribe remained loyal to him, however, and went with him to Brewer. Eventually the two men became reconciled, but the tribe resented the disunity caused by the quarrel, and at a conference in August, 1838, both men were deposed and two others appointed as Governor and Lieutenant Governor. The two old chiefs refused to abdicate, however, so that from 1838 there were two head chiefs and two second chiefs. Their respective adherents formed the Old Party and the New Party. The Government of Maine, fearing serious trouble would arise from this situation, planned in 1839 to change the election of Governor and Lieutenant Governor from life offices to biennial elective offices.

John Neptune could neither read nor write, but he realised the great importance of being able to do so. When he was in his eighties he was zealous in his pursuit of education for his people, and strongly supported the younger men of the tribe in their efforts. Fannie Hardy Eckstorm wrote that she gained the impression of Neptune that he was 'always essentially pagan, though the strong man of his tribe, who always stood for independence in thought and action. He was unwavering in his friendship for the white people and his advocacy of education for his people.'

Neptune returned to Indian Island in 1850, and Henry David Thoreau, who visited the Island in 1853, described in his book *The Maine Woods* a visit he paid Neptune. He wrote, 'We called on Governor Neptune who lived in a little "ten-footer", one of the humblest of them all . . . he was abed. When we entered the room, which was one half of the house, he was sitting on the side of the bed. He had a black frock-coat and black pants, much worn, white cotton shirt, socks, a red silk handkerchief about his neck, and a straw hat. His black hair was only slightly grayed. He had very broad cheeks, and his features were decidedly and refreshingly different from those of any of the upstart Native American party whom I have seen. He was no darker than many old white men. He told me that he was eighty nine, but he was going moose hunting that Fall, as he had done the previous one.' Thoreau wrote that various squaws hovered around during the visit, and that one sat on the bed by Neptune's side and helped him out with his stories. Thoreau described the squaws as 'remarkably corpulent, with smooth, round faces, apparently full of good humor.'

Toward the end of his life Neptune became almost blind, and was very feeble in mind and body. He had seen great social and economic changes in his long life-time. He was born in a birch bark wigwam with a fire in the centre on the bare earth, and his bed was of fir boughs covered with the skins of animals. He died in a frame house, with a bed and blankets, a stove and a clock. He wore clothes similar to those of the white men, ate their food and spoke their language. Many of the changes were not easy for some of the older Indians, who still preferred their old customs, and had never sat on a chair or used a table. Fannie Hardy Eckstorm recalled going to an Indian home with her father, where they were invited into the parlour. This had a good tapestry carpet, and the typical furnishings of a best room. However, the carpet was bundled in a heap on the floor in the middle of the room, with the furniture piled upon it. Fannie and her father were offered chairs, but the host and hostess squatted cross-legged on the floor.

John Neptune's death was hastened by the delusion, one Spring night, when he awoke feeling cold, that he was camping out, and that the fire had burned low. He pulled the straw bed from his bedstead into one corner of the room and set fire to it. He was nearly stifled by the smoke and died soon after. After his death, the tribe forgave and forgot the old Governor's stormy past, and remembered only his prowess as a hunter, his great ability as an orator, and his sagacity and courage. They honoured and revered his memory, and a monument in the cemetery on Indian Island is inscribed:

Lieut. Governor John Neptune
Born July 22, 1767
Died May 8, 1865
He held his commission as Lieutenant Governor for 50 years.

In the early 1960's an old Passamaquoddy Indian woman took to the tribal Governor, John Stevens, an old shoe-box containing documents that had been in her family for many years. The woman thought the documents might have historical significance, and that the tribe should have them. As he began to peruse the documents Governor Stevens was amazed. They told the history of dealings between the State of Maine, its predecessor, the Government of Massachusetts, and the Passamaquoddy Indians. The documents mentioned trust funds set aside for the Indians in exchange for land. Governor Stevens began investigations, and it was discovered that a six thousand acre tract of land known as Indian township had been taken from the tribes and the money, which was supposed to be in a trust fund, had lapsed into the State's general fund. Governor Stevens travelled to Augusta to ask State officials to give Indian Township back to the Indians, and to re-establish the trust fund. The State refused. More research was done, and it was discovered that a little known law called the Non-Intercourse Act had been passed in 1790 by the first United States Congress. This law said that in the thirteen original colonies, the Federal Government had to approve any land dealings between the states and the Indians. It said that transfers of title to Indian land were not valid unless approved by the Congress of the United States of America. One of the movers of the Non-Intercourse Act was a famous Maine citizen, Henry Knox, who was in George Washington's first Cabinet.

However, for some reason, Massachusetts, of which Maine was a part at that time, subsequently negotiated treaties with the Passamaquoddy and Penobscot Indians, involving the transfer of huge tracts of Indian land. Those treaties were never submitted for approval to the Congress. Subsequent transfers followed, and when Maine became a State in 1820, it assumed all of the obligations of the treaties that Massachusetts had entered into with the Indian tribes. It was assumed that those obligations were of services and payment of one kind or another that were provided in the treaties.

In 1972, the Passamaquoddies and Penobscots went to the Federal Government and asked the Department of the Interior to sue the State of Maine on the basis that Maine had violated the Non-Intercourse Act. United States District Judge Edward Gignoux made three important decisions:
  (1) That the Non-Intercourse Act did apply to the thirteen original states.
  (2) That the Federal Government which for two hundred years had refused to recognise the so-called State tribes as Federal obligations for the purposes of services and programmes (such as those provided for Indians in the West) had a similar obligation with respect to those tribes in Maine and the other original colonies.
  (3) That the Federal Government had a responsibility

as trustee of the Indians to represent the Indians in their claim under the Non-Intercourse Act.

This was a major victory for the Indians, and to demonstrate that they had won their case, they marched into Baxter State Park, a vast forested area in Northern Maine, and set up camp. They claimed that Mount Katahdin, Maine's highest mountain, had religious significance for them, and since it was only a matter of time before they won their case in court, they would take the land in the park immediately. The occupation ended with the State agreeing not to prosecute the Indians for trespass or for any other park rules they had violated. It soon became alarmingly clear what an enormous impact the case was going to have on the State as a whole, and on the fourteen major timberland companies, who owned vast areas of land which the Indians were now claiming. Construction of schools, municipal buildings and other projects came to a halt. A Boston-based firm refused to certify a 27 million dollar bond issue which the State had tried to float, saying that since there was a cloud on the title of much land in the State it could not be guaranteed that the State and municipalities could collect taxes on the lands, and might therefore be unable to pay off the bonds.

Originally the Indians were claiming 12½ million acres of land, approximately two thirds of the land area of the State, and 25 billion dollars in damages. They asked the President if he would appoint a task force or work group, so that they could present their view of what a reasonable settlement would be. This was done, and eventually, on October 10th, 1980, a settlement was signed in Washington by President Carter, using an eagle feather for a pen. The tribes got far less than they originally claimed. The settlement will provide them with a 27 million dollar trust fund, and an additional 54.5 million dollars with which to purchase 300,000 acres of forest land from a dozen major private timber management companies.

The tribes intend to purchase and operate two saw-mills and a blueberry farm within the 300,000 acres, which are scattered across the Northern section of the State. In this way it is hoped more jobs will be created, and the living standards of the people will be raised. So begins a new era for the Indian population of Maine.

An Indian Prayer

O great Spirit, whose voice I hear in the winds, and whose breath gives life to all the world, hear me.
I am small and weak; I need your strength and wisdom.
Let me walk in beauty, and make my eyes ever behold the red and purple sunset.
Make my hands respect the things you have made, and my ears sharp to hear your voice.
Make me wise so that I understand the things you have taught my people.
Let me learn the lessons you have hidden in every leaf and rock.
I seek strength, not to be greater than my brother, but to fight my greatest enemy: myself.
Make me always ready to come to you with clean hands and straight eyes.
So when life fades, as the fading sunset, may my spirit come to you without shame.

I feel Senabeh tried to live by these principles in his island retreat.

Chapter 3

Sir Ferdinando Gorges.

As I learned more about
Maine's early history it
seemed uncanny how sub-
tly interwoven it is with the
area in which I was born
and had spent my child-
hood and young woman-
hood. Plymouth, in the
county of Devon in Eng-
land, was the birthplace of
many great seamen and
explorers. Martin Fro-
bisher, a native of Ply-
mouth, sailed from that
port in 1576 in search of
the North West Passage.
Sir Francis Drake sailed

from Plymouth in 1577 on his voyage around the world,
and in 1582 Sir Humphrey Gilbert left there and founded
England's first colony in Newfoundland. It was from
Plymouth that in 1584 Sir Walter Raleigh recruited the
sailors for his ships and set sail for the New World in an
effort to plant an English colony there. In 1588, Sir
Francis Drake played his famous game of bowls on
Plymouth Hoe before sailing out of the harbour to help
defeat the great Spanish Armada which was rapidly
approaching England's shores. It was from Plymouth
Barbican, too, that the Mayflower set sail in 1620 with
the Pilgrim Fathers on their journey to a new life in the
New World.

As a child, one of my favourite outings was to cross
the River Tamar (the river dividing Devon and Cornwall)

by ferry, and go to Plymouth Hoe and the Barbican, to see the statue of Sir Francis Drake, and the Mayflower stone. Little did I ever dream that one day I should be living in a State in America which was founded by another man whose life was bound up in this city of Plymouth. This was Sir Ferdinando Gorges, who for many years was Commander of the Fort at Plymouth, and was a kinsman of Sir Walter Raleigh, another West Country hero. Every school child in England has heard of Sir Francis Drake and Sir Walter Raleigh, both famous Elizabethan heroes. Yet in spite of a life spent in equal service to his queen and country, their contemporary, Sir Ferdinando Gorges, remains unheard of, 'a prophet without honour in his own country.'

About six miles from the centre of Plymouth is Saint Budeaux Parish church. The existing church was built in 1563. Inside there is a monument which had been erected in 1600 by Tristam Gorges on top of the family tomb, to commemorate members of the Budokshed and Gorges families. The wording on the embellished reredos of slate reads 'Restored 1881, chiefly at the expense of the Historical Society and citizens of the State of Maine, U.S.A. in memory of Sir Ferdinando Gorges, the first Proprietor and Governor of that Province A.D. 1635, aided by some connections of the Gorges family in England.'

In 1963, in order to commemorate the fourth centenary of the church, a short history entitled *A Safe Stronghold* was written by I. F. Barnes. This abbreviated history is a fascinating one. Early in the fifth century, after the Romans had left Britain, the country was rapidly overrun by the invading armies of Jutes, Angles and Saxons, and the Celtic people were compelled to flee westward, taking refuge in Devon, Cornwall and Wales. The invading hordes largely wiped out the Christian Church in the areas which they conquered, and Thor and Wodin usurped the place of Christ. But in the West Country the

Church struggled on, strengthened by links with the Church and its leaders in Brittany and other parts of Gaul. One of these leaders was the missionary-minded Bishop Budoc of Dol. Budoc, grandson of the King of Brest, spent some of his childhood years in exile with his mother in Cornwall. On returning to Brittany the boy was baptized by the Abbot of a nearby monastery, and later became a monk himself. The details of his life are shrouded in legend, but it is known that he was Bishop of Dol for twenty years. He died at the age of eighty three in the year 500 A.D. and is buried in the Cathedral at Dol. It was about 480 A.D., over a hundred years before Saint Augustine built his first church at Canterbury, that a band of missionary monks sent out by Bishop Budoc crossed the English Channel in an open boat from Brittany, and sailed up the River Tamar, landing in the shelter of the Ernesettle Creek. There they formed a settlement and built a little wattle church. It was to this settlement and to other similar ones that the Bishop himself would have come from time to time to make his pastoral visits, and to encourage those whom he had sent out to preach and teach.

As time went by, wattle gave way to stone, and the first permanent stone church known to be dedicated to Saint Budoc was a small chapel built somewhere near the River Tamar some time before William the Conqueror invaded the country in 1066. It is not known where or when it was built. Local historians are still in dispute over the site, but it is fairly certain that it was close to the manor house. The church of Saint Budeaux (as it became known) did not become a Parish church until 1482. Until this time it was dependent for its ministry on the monks of Plympton Priory, and on St. Andrew's church, Plymouth, for the use of its cemetery. Those who lived in this area had no resident minister and had the inconvenience of having to make the 'hazardous journey' into Plymouth to St. Andrew's for burials. Thus in 1482, backed by John Stubbes, the vicar of St. Andrew's,

over twenty of the local people petitioned the Bishop of
Exeter that St. Budeaux should be a separate Parish, and
that a plot of land should be consecrated as a cemetery.
Their request was granted, and the Bishop decided that
four pence a year should be paid to the Prior, and forty
shillings a year to the vicar of St. Andrew's to compensate
him for the loss of revenue from burials.

The present church was completed in 1563, just five
years after the twenty five year old daughter of Henry
VIII and Anne Boleyn had become Queen of England,
and only nine years after the three great reformers of
the Church of England, Cranmer, Latimer and Ridley,
had been burnt at the stake during the reign of Mary.
There is no record of how money was raised for the
building of the church, but it is probable that it was
built largely through the generosity of Roger Budokshed
of Budokshed Manor. Roger Budokshed gave the piece
of land on which the church stands, to the churchwardens
and twenty four parishioners. He also gave them another
piece of land to the North-East of the church for the
period of two thousand years, on the condition that one
penny was paid to him and his heirs annually between
one o'clock and three o'clock on the afternoon of Christmas Day at the South door of the church.

During the Civil War in the reign when the King's
forces were struggling against the Parliamentary troops
under Oliver Cromwell, the church and churchyard
were used as a garrison by the Royalists. On April 16th,
1664, Lieutenant Colonel Martin, the officer in command
of the Parliamentary forces in Plymouth, heard that there
were five hundred Royalists at St. Budeaux, and sent
six hundred musketeers, who surprised the cavalier
garrison and captured two officers, forty four soldiers,
twenty horses, three barrels of powder, and over a
hundred weapons. Later the same year St. Budeaux
was once again the scene of heavy fighting, and after
an hour and a half of intensive battle the Roundheads

took the church and captured twenty one officers and one hundred soldiers. After the battle the church was little more than a wreck, and it was not until 1655 that it was restored.

Much of the history of the church.is linked with Budokshed manor and the Budokshed family and their successors. Budokshed manor is mentioned in the Domesday Book. The Budokshed family lived at the manor for thirteen generations until the time of Roger Budokshed, who gave the land for the second church. The estate passed to the Gorges family through Roger's daughter, Winifred, who married Sir William Gorges. Winifred was a cousin of Sir Humphrey Gilbert and Sir Walter Raleigh. Tristam, the son of Sir William Gorges and his wife, Winifred, was a veteran of the Spanish Armada victory. It was Tristam's daughter, Elizabeth, who later became Sir Ferdinando Gorges' third wife. When Gorges became Governor of the Plymouth Fort he bought a house at Kinterbury Creek, the next creek down river from Budokshed, and it is likely that he attended the church at St. Budeaux as a parishioner.

The keeping of registers at the St. Budeaux Parish church started in 1538 at the order of Thomas Cromwell, King Henry VIII's adviser, and apart from a break from 1660 to 1720, has been faithfully kept up ever since. The break in the registers occurred at a troubled time soon after the Civil War. The most notable entry is that of the marriage of Sir Francis Drake and Mary Newman in 1569.

Sir Ferdinando Gorges' appointment at Plymouth had thrown him into the company and friendship of his close relative, Tristam Gorges of Budokshed (Saint Budeaux), who was closely related on his mother's side to those intrepid voyagers, Sir Humphrey Gilbert and Sir Walter Raleigh. Gorges' own family and the men with whom he had associated for ten years before Captain George Weymouth sailed into Plymouth Harbour with his

Indian captives, were imbued with the spirit of American discovery, and Weymouth's arrival stirred Gorges' enthusiasm for exploration of the North American coast even further.

As a child I could see, from my bedroom window, part of the lovely grounds of Mount Edgcumbe, the large estate which had belonged to the Edgcumbe family for many centuries. Mount Edgcumbe, overlooking the entrance of Plymouth harbour, is one of the most attractive places in the area, and I have visited the grounds many times for garden parties. Little did I know then that an Elizabethan knight had granted to his friend and neighbour, Sir Richard Edgcumbe, three centuries earlier, on July 3rd, 1637, eight thousand acres of land in the State of Maine thousands of miles away. Nor did I ever dream that I would one day live in that State. Sir Richard Edgcumbe was one of the charter members of the Council for New England, and it has been claimed that this transaction between Gorges and Edgcumbe represented a full settlement of debts due to Sir Richard at that time. Edgcumbe lived only a year or two after the grant was made, so it is unlikely that he ever visited his new possession. Eighty one years after the date of the original grant was made, Nicholas Edgcumbe, supposed to be an heir, undertook to define the location and to establish the rights of other heirs to the tract of land known as Small Point, but by that time much of the territory had already been sold. However, the town of Edgcumb in Maine records the family name.

The present Earl of Mount Edgcumbe, in a letter to me, dated July 3rd, 1980, wrote that as a result of German bombing in March, 1941, Mount Edgcumbe had burned to the ground and all family records had been lost.

These, then, were some of the links which set me off on a fascinating search for more details of the Elizabethan knight, Sir Ferdinando Gorges, who was an earlier citizen of my own home town.

Sir Ferdinando Gorges' ancestry can be traced back to the time of the Norman conquest of Britain. His family took its name from a Norman parish on the coast of France. A knight named Ralph de Gorges held the parish of Gorges in Normandy. Apparently it was the struggle between the Angevin Dukes of Normandy and their overlord the King of France which uprooted the Gorges family and drove them to shelter in the English kingdom of their Norman lord. It would seem that Ralph de Gorges either came with William the Conqueror to England at the time of the Norman invasion in 1066, or followed soon afterwards. Two charters of William I in England in 1080 and 1082 were witnessed by a 'Ralph de Gorges.'

The Gorges family settled largely in Somerset, and during the Middle Ages played a part in the pageant of English history. In 1466, a Sir Thibault Gorges commanded at Rouen under the Duke of York, and his son Walter was a prominent adherent of the Yorkists during the Wars of the Roses. The family flourished in the 16th century, and a score of Gorges were to be found in high places. The most prominent and successful of these was Sir Thomas Gorges, who became a Groom of the Privy Chamber; as well as a trusted servant of Queen Elizabeth, he became her friend and emissary. He owed his long career in royal service to the fact that he never used his closeness to the Queen to further his own ambitions or to try to influence royal policy. Because of his influential position, however, Sir Thomas was able to further the career of his young kinsman, Ferdinando, the younger son of Edward Gorges. Edward came from the Wraxall (near Bristol, Somerset) branch of the family. He had died in 1566 when Ferdinando was only a few weeks old, and his brother, Edward, four years old. Very little is known about the early life and education of Ferdinando. It is known that his paternal grandmother,

Anne Walsh, had been tutored by William Tyndale (1494-1536), the English cleric who was the first to translate the Bible into English, and was later martyred for his Protestant views. If, as seems likely, Anne Walsh helped in Ferdinando's upbringing, it is not fanciful to see in her the source of Gorges' fervent Protestantism.

There is no doubt that the boys were given a good education. Edward, the older brother, went to Oxford before settling down to manage the Somerset estates he had inherited. It is possible that for a time Ferdinando may have studied at Oxford, too, and it is believed that he may have been attached to the Court for a time, as a page in the Queen's service. Certainly he must have been well-educated, as he wrote English with ease and fluency. As the younger son Ferdinando received a smaller inheritance. In his father's will, which had been made soon after his birth, he received a gold chain weighing twenty two ounces, one hundred pounds, and the manor of Birdcombe, which is close to Wraxall in Somerset. Following in the footsteps of his ancestors he became a professional soldier, with first-hand experience of soldiering in all its phases.

In the year before the Spanish Armada, Gorges took part in the defence of Sluis in the Netherlands, against the Spanish. It was this English interference which led in part to the launching of Philip of Spain's Armada against England in 1588. During the time of the Armada, Gorges was a prisoner of war in the hands of the Spanish, and did not return to England until late in 1588 or early 1589. Soon after this he married Anne Bell, daughter of Edward Bell in Essex. As her dowry she brought him various lands in Devonshire, Somerset and Gloucestershire. During the next few years Gorges fought in several campaigns on behalf of King Henry IV in Normandy, and in 1591 served with the Queen's favourite, the dashing young Earl of Essex, in the siege of Rouen. Gorges was knighted for the part he played in this campaign.

On his return to England Gorges settled down to family life. In 1593 his first son was born, and until 1595, his time was spent partly with his family and partly at Court in the Queen's service. During these years he developed his connections with the prominent men about the Court, such as Lord Burghley and his son, Robert Cecil, and strengthened his friendship with the Earl of Essex. About this time, at the Court, his kinsman, Sir Walter Raleigh, was a favourite, too.

During the 1580's there had been repeated alarms that the Spanish were preparing to invade England. The South West coast of England was the front line defence against the Spaniards, and the provision of defence for the coasts of Devon and Cornwall was imperative. The early Tudors had fortified Drake's Island, Plymouth (then known as St. Nicholas Island), in order to prevent a French invasion. With the increasing insecurity at this time, the Privy Council began to doubt whether these defences were adequate. The town of Plymouth also began to regard the island as insufficient protection, and asked for a garrison of one hundred men, and for the right to have Sir Francis Drake in command. Queen Elizabeth ordered the construction of a fort on the high South East corner of Plymouth Hoe, as a guard for the town and the Sound during this period of tension, and work was started in 1592. In July 1595, the Spanish alarmed the whole of England by landing in Cornwall, and burning Penzance and other nearby places. It was generally agreed that this could never have happened if the defences had been more adequate, and if there had been good leaders in the West Country to repel the invaders.

At this time Gorges was in Plymouth as a Commissioner to send off an expedition of Drake and Hawkins against the Spanish. Lord Burghley instructed him to report on the progress of the building of the Plymouth Fort. This he did, and it was decided that Gorges, an experienced soldier, was the man to take charge at

Plymouth. The people of Plymouth realised that their hopes of regaining control of the Fort themselves were to be thwarted, and they informed Lord Burghley of their displeasure at the appointment. It seems that the Plymouth men objected to the appointment of Gorges not so much because he was a stranger, but because he was outside their control, and primarily a royal servant. By February 1597 construction work on the Fort was substantially completed after five years of effort, and at a cost of just over two thousand pounds. This fortress was able to dominate the Sound with its guns, and could also guard the entrance to the inner harbour which lay beside the town.

Gorges was about thirty years of age when he was appointed Commander of this new fort at Plymouth. Unfortunately, from the beginning it was clear that the differences which had been revealed during the building of the fort were still preventing real co-operation. There were repetitions of the friction between fort and town, and it was clear in view of these disputes that in the event of an enemy attack Gorges might not receive the support of the armed strength of the town in time to be of use. Gorges was trying not to interfere with the liberties of the town of Plymouth. His sole concern was the danger of a Spanish invasion, and he endeavoured unceasingly to collect stocks of weapons, even to providing some of the munitions from his own private means.

A letter from William Stallenge of Plymouth to Sir Robert Cecil in May, 1598, reflected the town's antagonism. He wrote, 'The Townsmen hope some good course established between Sir Ferdinando Gorges and them,' and, referring to the billeting of troops in the town, he added, 'But it is here supposed to be a matter rather proceeding from Sir Ferdinando Gorges to show his good will toward the town. I would that Her Majesty would appoint him to some other place, for there will be no end of his malice, which will in this place greatly hinder her service.' The quarrel went to the Privy Council who ruled against Gorges in some respects, but empowered him to command the town and equipment when danger threatened.

Gorges continued faithfully doing his duty at Plymouth, but was hindered constantly by the fact that the State was unable to provide enough money to finance the fort. He was almost in despair at the miserable conditions of his troops, who were sorely neglected. They were destitute of money and adequate clothing, and in winter often lacked fuel and proper shelter. In letters to the Privy Council, Gorges wrote in the plainest terms of the desperate needs of the defensive forces, and of the futility and frustration of trying to defend the place without adequate supplies. In vain he appealed to the Government. It was bankrupt, and what was done for the defence of Plymouth had to be done by him and other patriotic subjects. Not only was the Treasury empty, but Gorges' own fortunes, or rather, those he had received through his marriage with Anne Bell, were being exhausted in trying to alleviate the misery of his soldiers. The State had been niggardly, too, in the supply of arms. A survey of the heavy artillery of the Plymouth Fort, which was made during the period of Gorges' later temporary removal from the Command, revealed the amazing fact that all the apparatus for the firing of the guns had been supplied by Gorges, and was his personal property.

At the beginning of 1601 while Gorges was at Plymouth feeling frustrated and dissatisfied by the inadequate preparations made to resist a Spanish attack, jealousies and disputes were seething at the Court around the ageing Queen. There was intense rivalry between the Earl of Essex, Sir Walter Raleigh, and Sir Robert Cecil for the Queen's favour. There was great uncertainty because of the unsettled question of the succession, and controversy, too, about the question of whether the long war with Spain should be brought to a negotiated peace. The Earl of Essex was leader of the party which wanted to continue the fight with Spain. He had been the Queen's favourite for a long time, and was also popular with the people. However, this growing popularity had aroused the suspicions of the Queen, who would permit no rival to her sovereignty. She had become apprehensive of his intentions, and his numerous enemies and rivals were only too ready to plan for his downfall, and whisper their poison against him. The Earl's Irish expedition in 1599 caused the final breach between the Queen and her impetuous favourite, and he was dismissed from the Court. At the end of 1600, Essex was still excluded from the Queen's presence, and blamed his rivals for this. His proud spirit sought revenge against those who plotted against him, and Essex House, his home in the Strand, became the meeting place for all kinds of people ready to assure him of their support. Swordsmen rode in from Wales; powerful nobles arrived, and preachers who harangued the crowds with strange doctrines which appeared to sanction the deposition of monarchs. Essex summoned to his side all those who he felt owed him allegiance. Gorges was one of these. Thus it was that, at the end of January, 1601, he received a letter from Essex telling him of the wrongs that had been heaped on his patron and friend, and urgently requesting him to be in London by February 2nd. In the mind of Essex this was not to be a revolt against the Queen, merely a plan to free her from her evil counsellors; his followers recognized the need for reform at this time and believed they were engaged in a righteous cause.

Arriving in London, Gorges was told by Essex and his supporters (about one hundred and twenty earls, barons, knights and gentlemen) of their plans, which involved an attempt on the Court and town. Gorges objected with good sense and caution that their forces were totally inadequate for such a great undertaking, and it was decided that the attempt should be made on the Court

alone. The Queen would then be forced to form a new
Council, and displace from office those who were hostile
to Essex. Gorges' sense of loyalty was shocked at the
idea of so forcing the Queen against her will, and he
objected to this plan also.

Gorges was actually under as much of an obligation to
Sir Robert Cecil as to Essex, and had always maintained
the closest relations with his kinsman, Sir Walter Raleigh.
They had co-operated in the defence of the West Country,
when Raleigh, as Lord Lieutenant of Cornwall and
Admiral of the West, was Commander in Chief of the
Naval and Military forces of Devonshire. Gorges, therefore, found himself in a very awkward position. In the
meantime, Raleigh was alarmed to learn that his own
kinsman was involved with this rebellious faction, and
sent a message asking Gorges to meet him at his home,
Durham House. However, on the instructions of Essex
it was agreed that the meeting should take place, instead,
in an open boat in the middle of the River Thames. So
it was that on a cold February day the two men talked
together as their boats jostled against each other on the
flowing tide. Raleigh told Gorges that there was a warrant
issued for his arrest, and urged him to return to his fort
at Plymouth, otherwise he would find himself in serious
trouble. The discussion ended abruptly when a volley of
shots rang out, and a boat containing four armed men
headed towards Gorges and Raleigh. There was no time
for further argument and Gorges pushed Raleigh's boat
away toward the opposite bank out of harm's way.
Raleigh realised from his conversation with Gorges the
imminent danger to himself and his friends at Court, and
hurried back to warn them. In the meantime a deputation
of Privy Councillors had gone to Essex House to read
the Riot Act, and had been detained as hostages. Raleigh
spent the rest of the day getting his men ready to defend
the Queen to the death. These precautions proved un-
necessary, as the Earl of Essex failed to get the support
he expected from the townspeople. Gorges quickly

realised that the coup was doomed to failure, and hurried back to Essex House. He released the Privy Councillors who had been held hostage since that morning and took them by boat to the Court. Still hoping for a peaceful solution he laboured faithfully to get the support of Raleigh and Cecil, hoping to obtain for Essex and his followers immunity from punishment. The plan failed and Gorges found himself a close prisoner in the Gatehouse prison, one of the worst prisons in London. There he was interrogated, and he gave information about the course of events after his arrival in London, and the discussions which had taken place. He felt that to have withheld these facts would have endangered his own life without benefiting Essex in the least.

Essex mistakenly thought that by releasing the hostages, and testifying under oath that he disapproved of the course Essex had taken, Gorges was a traitor. In the trial which followed, Essex showed his indignation at Gorges, and demanded to be brought face to face with him. Essex was condemned to death. Gorges was deeply grieved, and in his book *The Breefe Answer* wrote of Essex:

> Every man will keep company with such as he is himself; he was of the same profession that I was, and of a free and noble spirit. But I must say no more, for he is gone and I am here; I loved him alive, and cannot hate him being dead; he had some imperfections—so have all men; he had many virtues—so have few; and for those virtues I loved him; and when time which is the trial of all truths hath run his course, it shall appear that I am wronged in the opinion of this idle age.

Thus Gorges made no denial of his loyalty to his former friend, despite the fact that he himself lay in prison in disgrace, in disfavour with the Government, scorned by his former fellow conspirators, and in the shadow of the Queen's displeasure. Gorges contemplated unhappily the ruin of his career. He had lost the command of his fort at Plymouth. He was ill and penniless. He pleaded with Sir Robert Cecil to obtain a pardon. Eventually,

through his uncle Sir Thomas Gorges' efforts, Gorges
was freed and given into the custody of his brother,
Edward, on bail of one thousand pounds. The people of
Plymouth had raised money, too, for his defence. Gorges
was virtually a beggar, and dependent on his relatives
for everything. The Queen agreed to his pardon, but
never fully forgave those concerned with Essex in the
revolt. While she lived, Gorges had little hope of being
restored to royal service, although eventually he regained
his property and his freedom.

After Elizabeth's death, King James I opened his reign
by widely distributing offices and honours. On September
15th, 1603, a warrant was signed by the new king which
stated, 'For some displeasure conceived by the Queen,
our sister deceased, Sir Ferdinando Gorges was removed
from the charge of the new fort at Plymouth and of St.
Nicholas Island, and the same committed to Sir John
Gilbert. And since our coming to the Crown the said
Sir Ferdinando Gorges hath given such satisfaction in
the former matters as we have been moved to restore
him to that charge and to recompense Sir John Gilbert
otherwise, and have granted to the said Sir Ferdinando
Gorges our letters patent of the charge.'

This return to his command at Plymouth was to mark
the beginning for Gorges of a new and exciting interest.
Over the years, as Commander of the Fort at Plymouth
he had enjoyed the company and friendship of his close
relative Tristam Gorges of Budokshed (St. Budeaux).
Tristam was closely related on his mother's side of the
family to Sir Humphrey Gilbert and Sir Walter Raleigh.
Thus the members of his own family, and the men with
whom he had associated over the years, were imbued
with the spirit of American discovery. Obviously, Gorges,
too, must have discussed with Raleigh his attempt at
colonization in Virginia.

It was in 1605 that Captain George Weymouth, a well
educated man, a student of Mathematics, shipbuilding
and fortification, was engaged by the Earl of Southamp-

ton to explore the coast of New England, and to discover a place suitable for a plantation. The English knew that the French had become interested in establishing a claim in this new land and were determined to compete. In 1604 Pierre du Gast, Sieur de Monts, made a successful French settlement in Acadia, now Nova Scotia.

Weymouth put out to sea in 'The Archangel'. He first saw the coast of the New World near Cape Cod, but because of rocks and other hazards he dared not land there. Landing on an island now known as Monhegan, off the coast of what is now Maine, he put up a cross and took possession of the land in the name of his sovereign. James Rosier, who was the chronicler on the voyage, described Monhegan as an island 'woody, grown with firs, birch, oak and beech as far as we saw along the shore; and so likely to be within. On the verge grow gooseberries, strawberries, wild pease and wild rose bushes. The water issued forth down the rocky cliffes in many places; much fowl of divers kinds breed upon the shore and rocks. While we were on shore, our men aboard, with a few hooks, got above thirty great cod and haddocks which gave us a taste of the great plenty of fish which we found afterwards wheresoever we went upon the coast.' They also found the Indians, and when they set sail again for England, Weymouth and his men took five Indians with them as captives. They were Tahanedo (or Nahanda), Amoret, Skidwares, Maneddo and Saffacomoit.

Captain Weymouth sailed into Plymouth Harbour and was met by Gorges, who was greatly interested in all that Weymouth had to tell him. He took three of the Indians into his home, where he treated them with great kindness. He taught them to speak English, and they told Gorges of the great rivers, the forests and lakes, the different tribes of Indians, the wild beasts, the birds, the fish, and the climate. Gorges was fascinated by all that the Indians told him, and from then on became a leading spirit in furthering the colonization of this new land. He wrote, 'These captives must be acknowledged the means under God of putting on foot and giving life to all our plantations.'

In 1606 King James I granted the petition of Sir John Popham (Chief Justice of England) and Sir Ferdinando Gorges for exclusive rights to trade and settle the new lands in North America. Two companies were formed, since the merchants of London and Plymouth, who were rivals in trade, did not always get along together. The companies were called the Plymouth and London Companies. The Earl of Southampton joined the London Company, while Gorges and Popham were prominent members of the Plymouth Company. Settlements in Maine were to depend upon the Plymouth Company for their beginning, and upon Gorges' persistence in his endeavours when all others lost interest. James Phinney Baxter wrote of Gorges, 'In all his acts and in his various writings, his motives appear to have been elevated above the mercenary spirit of his trading compatriots. His zeal for discovery and colonization was always conspicuous, maintaining a clear glow even after the mists of age had gathered about him.'

In order to gain more detailed knowledge of the area before settlement, Gorges and Popham sent out ships on two exploratory voyages to the New England coast. The captains, Hannam and Pring, decided that the mouth of the Sagadahoc River (later known as the Kennebec) was a good place for settlement, and after carefully noting the location they sailed for home. Popham and Gorges decided they now had sufficient information to send colonists into their grant. They were anxious to gain a foothold in the new land as soon as possible, as they had heard that the French were already attempting to settle and claim the land which King James had granted the Plymouth Company.

In May, 1607, two ships, the 'Gift of God' commanded by George Popham, a nephew of Sir John, the Chief

Justice, and the 'Mary and John' under the command of
Raleigh Gilbert, son of Sir Humphrey Gilbert, sailed from
Plymouth with about one hundred colonists. They reached
their destination in early August and chose a site for
settlement not far from the mouth of the river. The land
was strange, with dense, dark forests filled with wild
animals and other unknown hidden dangers. The colonists set to work immediately felling trees to build houses
and a sturdy pinnace of thirty tons which they named the
'Virginia'. Presently the Winter was upon them, and they
soon found that the severity and length of the Maine
Winter was something for which they were totally unpre-
pared. They had never experienced such bitterly cold
weather, and their clothing and shelter were quite
inadequate for such conditions.

The elected Governor of the colony, George Popham,
was a man of middle age, 'fat, timorous, and incom-
petent.' Raleigh Gilbert has been described as a young
man of twenty four, 'with little zeal for religion, head-
strong, and of small judgement.' During the months
which followed, the colonists suffered great hardship.
There was illness, shortage of food, and a serious fire
which destroyed some of the buildings containing the
colonists' essential supplies. Everything seemed against
them. George Popham, in the terrible conditions, became
ill and died, and when the supply ship arrived in the
Spring, bringing fresh supplies of tools, arms, and
provisions, the colonists were ready to abandon the
colony. The Captain of the supply ship also bore the
news of the death of the Chief Justice, Sir John Popham,
and the death, too, of Raleigh Gilbert's elder brother.
This meant that as Gilbert was now the heir to large estates in England, he felt compelled to return in order to
take charge of his inheritance. All the colonists were
eager to leave the area and set sail thankfully for England. On their return they described the country as unfit
for human habitation, cold, barren and inhospitable.
Gorges summed up his great disappointment over the

failure of the colony in the words, 'All our hopes were frozen to death.' It was this settlement, however, at the mouth of the Sagadahoc (Kennebec), although temporary, which formed the basis of the English claim to New England, and was admitted as such by France, the rival claimant.

Gorges refused to admit defeat and soon regained his confidence in the new country. During the next few years he planned and sent out other expeditions. In 1614 Captain John Smith led an expedition, underwritten by certain London merchants, to the coast of Maine to hunt for gold and copper mines, catch whales, fish, and trade for furs. As he went he carefully mapped the region in such exact detail that the sites he described can be recognised to this day. Smith returned to England convinced that this region was eminently suitable for colonization, and that fishing and fur trading would be more profitable than mining. Although he managed to further attempts at colonization, a series of mishaps frustrated his hopes each time the venture was attempted. No other Englishman of that age was more fascinated by the spirit of adventure which prevailed then than Gorges. He threw himself wholeheartedly into these early attempts to explore and colonize, and exhausted his fortune on these enterprises.

Gorges had married four times, and each of his marriages had brought him large estates and great wealth. His first marriage to Anne Bell had lasted thirty years, and he claimed that he had spent much of the fortune she had brought to the marriage on the efficient running and maintenance of the Plymouth Fort. His second marriage, in December, 1621, was to Mary Achim, who was the widow of Thomas Achim of Cornwall. Again he used money from her estates for his New England ventures. After Mary's death in 1622 he remained alone for several years. Then in 1627 he married Elizabeth, the daughter of his old friend and kinsman, Tristam Gorges of Budokshed (St. Budeaux). Unfortunately, Elizabeth lived for only a short time after the wedding, and once more Gorges was left a widower. On September 21st, 1629, he married another cousin, Elizabeth, the daughter of Sir Thomas Gorges, the uncle who had been of such great assistance to him over the years. Elizabeth was the widow of Sir Hugh Smyth of Ashton Court near Bristol. This fourth marriage made it possible for Gorges to retire from the Plymouth Fort and to devote the rest of his life to his great dream of colonization. Lady Gorges, though tolerant of her husband's tremendous enthusiasm, was less hopeful of success in this venture. In a letter to her son, Thomas, she wrote, 'I must thank you for your love and care of the old man. Saturday last, his New England people set sail. God speed them well for I have little hope of any success.'

Between 1625 and 1630 wars with France and Spain, and the resultant responsibilities at home gave Gorges little opportunity to attend to New England settlements. In 1629 the war with France came to an end, and negotiations eventually led to peace with Spain. After the death of James I, Charles I succeeded to the throne. In 1629, too, trouble had arisen between the King and Parliament, and between Puritans and Episcopalians. Charles angrily dissolved Parliament, and for eleven years until the Long Parliament met in 1640 he ruled the country alone. Gorges was fully committed on the side of the King, and he remained zealous in his devotion to the monarchy and the established church.

Many of the Plymouth Company members gradually became discouraged and lost interest, but Gorges still persevered with singleminded devotion and dedication toward his goal. He wrote, 'I dealt not as merchants or tradesmen are wont, seeking only to make mine own profit, my ends being to make perfect the thorough discovery of the country, as I opened the way for others to make their gaine which hath been the meanes to encourage their followers to prosecute it to their own advantage. Were the strength of my body and meanes answerable to my heart, I would undertake the discovery of the utmost extent thereof.'

In 1620 Gorges had succeeded in obtaining a new patent for a group which was to succeed the Plymouth Company, and became known as the Council for New England. A distinguished list of peers and gentry from the West of England were among its members. When he had been summoned before the House of Commons to answer charges made against the Council, Gorges reminded them of his unstinted labours, and of the discouragement and disappointment suffered by the Council. He said, 'I have spent twenty thousand pounds of my estate, and thirty years in new discoveries and settlements upon a new continent.' He pointed out, too, that the Council members could show that their disbursements had far exceeded their receipts. The Council held its last meeting on April 25th, 1635, when only sixteen members were present. The cause of the dissolution was recorded as follows: 'We have been bereaved of friends, oppressed with losses, expenses and troubles; assailed before the Privy Council again and again with groundless charges, and weakened by the French without and within the realm. What, therefore, now remains is only a breathless carcass. We therefore now resign the patent to the King, first reserving all grants by us made and all vested rights.'

The Council officially surrendered its charter to the King on June 5th, 1635, and part of the new arrangement was that Gorges was to become Governor General of all New England. There was consternation in Massachusetts at this proposal, and the authorities there were determined to prevent this at all costs. Maine, though sparsely settled and inferior in strength to Massachusetts, was always 'a thorn in the flesh' and they knew, too, that Charles had expressed his intention of making Maine the seat of his authority. In the meantime, Gorges had named his tract in Maine, New Somersetshire, after his

own county seat in England, and sent his nephew,
William Gorges to govern there. William set up his
government in 1636, and opened a court there at Saco.
About this time, Gorges decided he must visit the place
he had fought so hard to develop. Unfortunately he was
destined never to see the land of his hopes and dreams,
as the ship in which he was to sail was completely dis-
abled in the launching, and events during the following
years would ensure that he would never be able to visit
Maine.

At last in 1639, after a delay of four years, King Charles
I granted to Gorges his celebrated charter for his Province
of Maine, so called, it is believed, as a compliment to
the wife of Charles I, Henrietta Maria, who was French,
and who owned as her private estate a province of France
known as the Province of Meyne. Gorges had failed to
become Governor General of New England, but so far
as his beloved province was concerned he had reached
the fulfillment of his desires. In this charter of Maine the
powers given to Gorges exceeded any which had ever
been granted by a sovereign to a subject. Gorges had the
right to appoint the clergy, could consecrate new
churches, could pardon offenders, proclaim martial law,
and maintain a standing army. Gorges proceeded to put
into execution his idea of a model government. It was
based on that of a Saxon Palatinate, and the Province of
Maine was divided into eight bailiwicks or districts, and
these in turn subdivided into hundreds, parishes and
tithings. Gorges, as Protector of the Faith, established
the Episcopal Church in Maine. There was none of the
narrow-minded bigotry that was so marked in Puritan
Massachusetts, and religious persecution was unknown.
Clergymen of any denomination were welcome, and
free to preach wherever they pleased.

In 1640, Gorges, still unable to leave England, and by
now an elderly man, appointed his cousin, Thomas
Gorges, Deputy Governor and Keeper of the Provincial
Seal. Thomas, a lawyer by profession, was liberal minded

and had an attractive personality. He governed the province wisely and well, and did a great deal to bring law and order to Maine. The affairs of the State were conducted with high moral standards, and Thomas Gorges was highly regarded by all. In his history, *The Beginnings of Colonial Maine, 1602-1658* (1914), Henry S. Burrage said of him, 'From first to last he had the respect of all law-abiding citizens. The three years he spent from 1640-1643 were passed in a way not only exceedingly creditable to himself, but helpful to the settlers in their desire to secure better conditions; and his name deserves to be accorded high honour for the services he rendered at an important period in the beginning of Colonial Maine. It is not too much to say of Thomas Gorges that his was by far the one conspicuously attractive personality in the province in all its early history.'

In 1641, the capital city, Gorgeana, was incorporated. It was located at Agamenticus (Indian for "the other side of the river") and was later renamed York. This was the first incorporated city in America. It had a mayor, with aldermen and councillors. There were two courts, one of which had sittings twice a year, and the other, for minor affairs, had weekly sessions. The city had a corporate seal, had powers to erect fortifications, and was authorized to become the seat of a Bishop of the Church of England.

In England, in the meantime, the King and Parliament were growing increasingly bitter toward each other, and civil war was brewing. Always a devoted servant of the King, and despite the fact that he was now an old man, Gorges upheld the King's cause. Thomas Gorges returned to England, leaving Richard Vines to carry on the government in the province. Unlike his cousin, Thomas was in sympathy with the Parliamentary forces. However, he did not hold any conspicuous position, either military or civil until 1649, when he was made

Lieutenant Colonel of a cavalry regiment in the Somerset militia. Both before and after the Restoration he was elected as Member of Parliament for Taunton, in Somerset. He lived an honoured and useful life at Heavitree, near Exeter in Devon, where he died on October 17th, 1670.

The Civil War destroyed all that Gorges had ever struggled to achieve, and had worked for and dreamed of for so many years. Oliver Cromwell's forces triumphed everywhere. Gorges was involved in the defence of Bristol with the King's forces. He was taken prisoner, thrown into prison, and all his property and lands confiscated. He was eventually released from prison, and returned to his home at Ashton Court in Somerset, where he died in 1647. In 1649, King Charles I was beheaded, and the Puritans under Cromwell gained control of England. Gorges' heirs, who were Royalists also, were unable to assert their claims in America, and the hopes of the Puritans to control the Maine colony arose. Commissioners were sent from Massachusetts to negotiate with the Maine authorities, but for a time the colonists resisted, feeling that Massachusetts had no right to claim Gorges' province. However, as the years passed, Massachusetts' leaders were troubled at Maine's vulnerability to attack by the French. They were appalled, too, at the growing lawlessness of the trading posts, and sent officers to Maine stating their right to govern. The Maine people were divided, but the majority wanted a strong government and protection from the French and Indians, and so voted to accept the control of Massachusetts.

Upon the restoration of Charles II to the English throne in 1660, a grandson of Gorges claimed Maine as his inheritance, and four years later a royal order commanded that Massachusetts should restore the province to Gorges' heir. Eventually in 1677, Gorges' grandson, Ferdinando, finally sold to Massachusetts all rights to Maine for the paltry sum of one thousand, two hundred and fifty pounds.

James Phinney Baxter, at the end of his book *Sir Ferdinando Gorges and his Province of Maine* (1890), sums up most aptly the high regard in which Gorges was held:

It is remarkable that so few memorials of a man so prominent as was Sir Ferdinando Gorges are to be found outside his own writings, which of course, present to us but a faint view of him. Yet he has left enough behind to show that he was a man of broad and beneficent views, intent upon benefiting his fellow-men, not only in his day and generation, but also by leaving behind him words which should redound to the welfare of posterity. We may see, also, that he was a man possessing the courage of his convictions: brave, sober, and wise in counsel; a staunch friend and generous enemy, since in his writings no word of criticism or ill feeling related to those who opposed him can be found. His mind was too much occupied with useful duties to permit him to waste time upon the plots, rivalries and enmities which surrounded him, and filled up the measure of some men's lives to the exclusion of better things. For more than forty years of his life he had ever before him the glowing vision of a new world, teeming with possibilities of good to mankind without number and without limit, and awaiting only the advent of willing spirits to become the theatre of achievements beyond all that man has yet attained. Such a prospect must have broadened his outlook upon the world, and ennobled his spirit. The words with which he closed his 'Narration' tell us this and will serve as a fitting termination to this fragmentary sketch of his life.

'. . . But I end, and leave all to Him who is the only author of all goodness, and knows best His own time to bring His will to be made manifest, and appoints His instruments for the accomplishment thereof; to whose pleasure it becomes every one of us to submit ourselves, as to that mighty God and gracious Lord, to whom all glory doth belong.'

Sir Ferdinando Gorges was a gallant, chivalrous knight, who built better than he ever knew, and I am glad as a fellow citizen of his former home in Plymouth, England, and having lived as a resident alien in his Province of Maine, to have learned these things about him, and, in turn, hope to make his contribution better known.

Chapter 4

West Country Adventurers.

In the year 1623, Christopher Levett, of Somerset, England, and a member of the Council for New England, crossed the Atlantic in order to survey suitable  areas for settlement in Maine. He kept a journal describing his travels and his impressions of Maine, and this was printed in London by a William Jones, and sold by Edward Brewster at the Sign of the Bible, in St. Paul's Churchyard, London in 1628. This journal is an extremely rare book, and the original copy is in the library of the New York Historical Society. The work relates almost wholly to the coast of Maine at an extremely early period, and provides a glimpse into the early history of the state. *A Voyage into New England* is Levett's diary of his travels which began in 1623 and ended about a year later.

Levett described his meeting with Governor Robert Gorges and other early settlers. He visited the area of the River Agamenticus and saw the potential of a good settlement there. It had, he wrote, good harbours for ships, good soil and timber. No attempt had been made as yet in that area, and it was not until 1630 that the first settlement at Agamenticus, now York, was made.

Levett wrote of his visit to Sawco (Saco) where he and his men were compelled to stay for five days, as apparently the weather conditions were too rough for them to continue by sea. During that time they lived in a wigwam type of shelter, which consisted of a few poles tied together, and covered with the sails from the boats. The weather continued to be bad for the whole of those days, with fog and rain and then snow. However, they had plenty of wood for their fires, and plenty of good fresh water for drinking. They had, too, abundant supplies of crane, geese, ducks, and other fowl which they boiled and roasted. They spread long, dry grass on the floor of the wigwam, and so were fairly comfortable, in spite of the conditions outside.

Levett wrote of his meeting with numerous Indians during his travels, and described how he had seen the Indians take their children and bury them up to the neck in the snow, in order to make them able to withstand the cold. When they were about two years old they would be thrown into the sea to teach them how to swim.

Levett wrote of the abundance of fish and deer in the state. He described the vines, the plum trees, the strawberries, raspberries, the walnuts and other varieties of nuts, as well as the great quantities of herbs, such as sassafras, sarsaparilla and aniseed. There was, he wrote, good soil for meadow land, pasture and corn, as well as clay, sand, gravel and rich black earth suitable for crops.

Having described the assets of the Maine area, Levett now wrote of some of the disadvantages.

'About the middle of May you shall have little flies, called musketoes, which are like gnats; they continue, as I am told, until the last of July. They are very troublesome for the time, for they sting exceedingly both by night and day. But I found by experience that boots or thick stockings would save the legs, gloves the hands, and tiffany [a kind of thin, transparent silk or muslin] or some such thing, which will not much hinder the sight, will save the face, and at night, any smoke will secure a man. The reason of the abundance of these creatures, I take to be the woods, which hinders the air, for I have observed always when the wind did blow but a little, we were not much troubled with them.

'Another evil or inconvenience I see there. The snow in winter did lie very long upon the ground.'

Levett, urging his countrymen in England to settle in this new land, wrote,

'I would to God that some one shire or more would begin this godly and profitable course. For certainly, God hath created all for the use of man, and nothing hath he created in vain. And if we will endure poverty in England wilfully, and suffer so good a country as this to lie waste, I am persuaded we are guilty of a grievous sin against God, and shall never be able to answer it.'

Levett urged that the nobles and rich merchants who had been abundantly blessed by God should join together and contribute money to help and train the poor for some skill whereby they might settle in the new land. However, he stressed the necessity for hard work, and laid down several stipulations that any considering the big step of emigrating to this new land should consider:

1. That it is a country where none can live except he either labor himself, or be able to keep others to labor for him.
2. If a man have a wife and many small children, not to come there, except for every three loiterers he have one worker; which if he have, he may make a shift to live and not starve.
3. If a man have but as many good laborers as loiterers, he shall live much better there than in any place I know.
4. If all be laborers and no children, let him not fear but to do more good there in seven years than in England in twenty.
5. Let no man go without eighteen months' provision, so shall he take the benefit of two seasons before his provision be spent.
6. Let as many plant together as may be, for you will find that very comfortable, profitable and secure.

Paul Coffin was descended from an old Devonshire family in England. His ancestors first came to America from England in 1642. Paul was born at Newbury, Massachusetts, in 1737 and spent his youth there. He was the seventh child of Colonel Joseph Coffin. Paul Coffin graduated from Harvard University in 1759, where he 'was noted and distinguished for his literary acquirements and correct deportment.' After graduation he taught school in Kingston, New Hampshire, and then at

Wells and Biddeford in Maine. Early in 1761 he commenced his ministry at Narragansett, now Buxton, Maine.

This young man, born and educated into a polished and literary society was, therefore, plunged into a bleak, uncultivated wilderness of a parish of less than thirty families, not one of whom was educated, and who lived in rough log cabins. His ordination was in the depths of Winter, and in that particular year it seemed that an unusually great quantity of snow fell, making travelling almost impossible.

On the day before the ordination, the Reverend Moses Morrill of Biddeford, with the delegates of his church, the Reverend Daniel Little and the Reverend Moses Hemmenway from Wells, together with other ministers and delegates of their respective churches, set out to walk on snow-shoes to the church. Unfortunately the snow was so deep that all the usual landmarks had been obliterated. The party soon realized that they were lost and had to remain in the woods all night, huddled together for warmth. Eventually, suffering from cold, hunger, and lack of sleep, they at last managed to reach the settlement the next day, just in time to complete the ordination services.

A classmate of Paul Coffin's, who was present on this occasion, wrote, 'I pitied brother Paul, whose education and social qualities fitted him to enjoy, if not to adorn, the most cultivated and polished society; that he should have his lot cast in that then forbidding field of labor, for I know that he would have given all that he then had, or ever expected, of this world's goods, to have avoided it; but the settlers and proprietors were unanimous that he should remain, and the path of duty appeared plain, which, however rugged, he never refused to enter, for brother Paul was a conscientious man.'

Within a year of his ordination Coffin married Mary Gorham of Charlestown, Massachusetts. Mary was a woman 'of good sense and accomplished manners.'

Her influence in the town and parish was great, and she supported her husband in all his ministerial labours. They had fourteen children. Mary taught her daughters all the arts of cooking, and the important and necessary arts of carding, spinning and weaving.

The first meeting house at Buxton was constructed of logs. Another meeting house was built in 1760, and this remained until after Coffin's death. This had plank seats laid on blocks of wood. It was not until the year 1790 that the meeting house was renovated and pews were installed. Coffin's salary was to be fifty pounds a year, and sixty acres of land, with a pledge for reasonable additions to the salary for necessary expenses. Another sixty acre lot was provided for the parsonage. It seems that around 1722 some difficulty arose regarding the payment of the minister's salary. Coffin, it appears, had been forced to spend much of his time growing crops to support and feed his growing family. He was then accused of neglecting the ministry. Eventually a compromise was reached, and it was agreed to pay Coffin's salary, partly in money, partly in corn, grain, and other produce, and partly in labour.

In that same year, 1722, Narragansett No. 1 was incorporated as Buxton by the General Court of Massachusetts. It was so called from the town of Buxton in England, and the name had been suggested by Coffin.

Paul Coffin was a learned man, familiar with Greek, Latin, Hebrew and French. He was a student throughout his life. His sermons were argumentative and earnest, and were delivered with an eloquence and emphasis of manner which kept the congregation attentive until the end of the sermon. Every sermon was well prepared, and after the subject had obviously been fully considered.

Coffin was a fine looking man of medium stature. He was erect and had a good physique. His face expressed his intelligence and gentleness, and his natural dignity and kindness won the love of all who knew him. He was sought after and admired by all who met him, and he conversed 'with ease and elegance'. His contemporaries in civil life felt refreshed and better people for his company. Coffin's most intimate friends among the clergy were those noted for their learning and piety. He was said to be exact and punctual in all his transactions, and honourable in all his dealings. Although he rather avoided than sought distinction, his scholarship became well known, and in 1812 the title of Doctor of Divinity was conferred upon him by Harvard University.

Paul Coffin died at the age of eighty four, after more than sixty years as a minister of the Gospel, a life spent in serving God and his fellow men well and faithfully.

In 1796, 1797 and 1798, Coffin made three missionary tours to various parts of Maine, each of them lasting about two months. During these periods he rode hundreds of miles on horseback over rough terrain and across rivers, to scores of small, scattered communities. He stayed at the homes of a great number of people, preached hundreds of sermons, and handed out hundreds of religious tracts.

Extracts from Coffin's journal are illuminating, and give us today a vivid picture of the ruggedness of life in those early days, both for the minister and his parishioners:

Raymondton
> They allowed my doctrine to be good, and me a good man, but not a preacher, as I read my sermons.

Philips Gore
> Heard a Mr. Stephen Hall, a Methodist. His sermon was juvenile, not accurate or instructive either in language or sentiment. Mercy in pardon and grace in sanctification were strongly blended. His grammar and pronunciation were bad. Instruction was imperfectly given and sound knowledge evidently wanting.

Paris
> Preached all one Sabbath day to about three hundred people, very attentive, decently dressed and well behaved; the largest and most hopeful assembly to which I have as yet spoken.

Hebron

Heard the Methodist, Mr. Stephen Hall, who preached from Isaiah 40,31—a very lean discourse from an excellent text.

Buckfield

Stayed at the home of a Mr. George Buck, who with nothing but his hands has advanced to five hundred acres of good land. He has eight pails of milk from ten cows.

Turner

Turner is beautiful, but dispirited in religion, tired of its minister, and vexed by a party of Baptists and its own covetousness.

Littleboro

I conversed with the people, who seemed to understand me, and rejoiced in plain and weighty truths, and to see through many delusions of the present day. A good meeting. One man raises annually about five hundred bushels of bread and fourteen hundred weight of flax.

Monmouth

Stayed with Colonel Chandler, a kind and pretty man, in a noble house, pleasantly situated. Small audience, the people being busy in the highways and raisings.

Mt. Vernon

Visited a Mrs. Daniels, long sick and emaciated, yet under hopes of recovery. Gave her advice and prayers. This is a place of horse jockeying, taverning, Law suits, etc. not affording hearers even for Baptists and Methodists.

Goshen

Preached from Titus 2, 14. Had a sweet, attentive audience, and two women especially, whose voices added to the beauty and force of the music, and raised my devotion.

New Sharon

Visited a Mrs. Gordon and a Mrs. Fulsom, their husbands being absent. They rejoiced and were thankful for the books given them. Mrs. Fulsom, especially, was mightily pleased to see a Congregational minister and nearly raptured.

New Vineyard

The house where I stayed was constructed of logs and bark.

At the South end of the house there was a sweet little bedroom, well furnished and admirably pleasing. In this rural arch of New Vineyard I slept sweetly after a night of fleas. There is a lovely spring near the house, ever flowing.

Sandy River area

Stayed at the home of the Withams, a very serious family. Family worship, consisting of reading, singing and praying was performed with much solemnity and religious thanksgiving.

Everywhere he went, Coffin was impressed by the industry and success of most of the people in their development of the land and the raising of crops. In his diary he wrote great details of the amounts of grain raised, for example, 'he has a pretty farm, has raised one hundred and twenty bushels of rye on three acres, from three bushels of seed', and 'a Mr. Carlisle had ninety two bushels of rye for two.'

Fairfield

Preached to a serious and considerable assembly, who were delighted and entertained. No people were more respectful or more pleased. They seemed to mix with their esteem, piety and sweet surprise. There seemed to be a holy awe among them and a joyful surprise at a visit of Gospel light and grace.

My sermon gave much satisfaction to the hearers, if we except a Mrs. Noble, a Baptist; she called it 'nothing but dishwater.'

Clinton

Rode two miles to Captain Jonathan Philbrick's in Sebasticook, just above the falls where they catch herring and shad. Thousands of barrels of herring have been taken this Spring. They put four quarts of salt to a barrel of them, and when salted enough they smoke them. Mr. Hudson had three thousand of them hanging over one's head in his shop or smoke house. A pretty sight. Near Mr. Hudson's house on the Kennebec are three double saw mills. Sixty king's masts have been hauled in his vicinity this year, and many of a less sort.

Sheepscot Ponds

Preached to a great assembly, all serious and very attentive.

The people were charmed and astonished to find the difference between the preaching of the standing clergy and illiterate teachers. Mr. Bradstreet was so affected with joy to have the people hear just such preaching as he had been wishing for, that tears prevented his power of speaking to me more than once.

Set off for Belfast in the company of one man—rode through woods about fifteen miles, from twelve to six of the clock. This land is excellent and the road not very good, being only cleared of wood by General Knox. We crossed the West and East branches of George's River; we found one house in about the middle of this fifteen mile road. This is owned by a Mr. Braddock of Great Britain. His pleasant little Dutch wife, being only at home, told us of her solitary situation, and of her sufferings in the necessary absence of her husband, with a peculiar sweetness of temper, and with all the calmness of a philosopher.

Belfast

Stayed at Northport with James Nesmith, a mile or two from Belfast. A fine prospect; a little river has a bridge over it close by the bay. The boats for the bay paddle under the bridge, and come at once to a side-mill. You see Blue Hill from here, and the vessels passing up and down almost without intermission.

Duck-trap (Lincolnville)

Preached to about ninety people. I was the first missionary ever to visit them. Stayed at the home of Squire George Ulmer. The Squire and his very comely wife treated me with a liberal hospitality. We had bloated eels, pigeons, fresh mackerel, cucumbers, wine, etc. We had no prayers the first night or morning at the Squire's. Saturday night I brought on the matter as delicately as possible. It took well. The Squire was submissive as to the morning and evening prayers, and respectful in the business altogether.

There were three families of Indians here, one from Canada, two from Penobscot. They were employed in felling trees, catching eels, making baskets, etc. I visited one family, and a young squaw and some little folks only in the tent. While I was sitting and talking with my young lady, an old squaw came in and said I was no minister in such a situation, but a young squire.

Warren

Dined at the home of General Knox. The General has a garden fenced ovally. Indeed, circles and semi-circles in his fences, etc. seem to be all the mode here. His house draws air beyond all the ventilators which I had before seen. I was almost frozen for three hours before we took dinner and plenty of wine. The General being absent I dined with Mrs. Knox and her daughters, and Mrs. Bingham and her sister and daughter. We had a merry dinner, the little misses talking French in a gay mood. Mrs. Bingham was sensible, had been in France, could talk of European politicks, and give the history of the family of the late king of France, and so on. The General's house, with double piazzas round the whole of it, exceeded all I had seen.

Union

Put up with Josiah Robbins nigh the meeting house. He took yesterday morning twenty four dozen pigeons in a net at once; and this morning seventeen dozen. Land here is very good at two dollars the acre, and a market is ready for ten times the produce now raised; a good place for young men to make themselves. We dined on pork and pigeons, with excellent potatoes and boiled corn and squash. Preached at four o'clock to about sixty or seventy hearers. The people were affected and thankful, particularly my host, Josiah Robbins, who was reverentially and solemnly affected with the truth, and deeply grateful. Duty done gives comfort. I thought in the morning it would be hardly worth the time and pains to aim at a lecture in Union. But I rejoice that I had visited the place, a town of serious lovers of good ministers and sound doctrine.

Wiscasset

A place of much trade and navigation with eight or ten majestic houses and many decent houses of a common two story size.

Bath

Bath is unhappily, half for their minister, Wallace, and half against him. The opposing half have the meeting house half the time for the Methodists. A miserable affair.

Sandy River Area

The River sends two or three thousand bushels of grain to market annually. A Mr. Church conveys from a hill to his house, water in pipes under ground. He turns a cock in his kitchen and chamber and draws it. A trough for cattle stands on the pipes and the water for them comes into it through a goose quill. The work cost one hundred dollars. Much sugar is made on this river and all around.

Greenfield

Captain Gray has a grand farm and much interval with corn to the acre. I rode in company with Benjamin Hilton of Wiscasset. He was taken by the Indians in 1756 at Pownalboro' and carried to Canada. His father, one brother and one brother in law were killed, and Benjamin alone taken prisoner. Captain Gray is like old Esop in body and mind; round in his shoulders, and of a witty turn of thought.

Carrytunck Falls

The people here are much reformed. Formerly they lived in strife, excess in drinking and shooting on the Lord's day, etc. These vile practices are now forsaken. The people are serious and thoughtful of religion, yet puzzled by different preachers; however, they seem teachable and modest.

Seven Mile Brook

Preached at Mr. Moore's to three or four hundred people. After service visited an infirm man, Mr. Fling. Many persons have been hurried into the water (baptized) in this place by Mr. Locke of Chester, near Sandy River. They are left as sheep without a shepherd.

Twenty five mile Pond
and Fifteen mile Stream

Rode to the last place and lodged at Mr. Fyle's. Thomas Gilpatrick and his wife who were neighbours, spent the evening with us. Our conversation was religious and instructive. Mrs. Gilpatrick said 'The people here are of two sorts; one swallows all kinds of preaching; the other, sick of false religion, have grown indifferent, even to the true.' If I understand Mr. Gilpatrick, the people here, taught by the predestination Baptists, suppose they may as well live in open sin as not. He said they were left in an awful situation.

Summing up this mission, Coffin wrote:

A great many of the people to whom I preached and gave private instruction, appeared teachable and all respectful. The youth have small means of Christian knowledge in private; and their

preachers, travelling, preach very differently. 'Tis as much to be
lamented in Maine perhaps, as anywhere, that people lack good
Christian education. For want of early and sufficient information
as to the leading truths and duties of the Gospel, they are in
danger of lasting ignorance of them; and of receiving error, and
of turning religion into a matter of hurtful and doubtful disputa-
tion. Better measures to promote the kingdom of Christ, and
more scriptural, are much wanted in this country in general;
and I believe, in all Christendom.

Later journal entries read:

Buckfield-mills

All preaching is thought by many here to be needless; and the
'Age of Reason' is too sweet to the people. Oh! the bad effects
of lay teachers of several sorts, and of deitistical writers,
when these follow as here, great ignorance and neglect of the
means of grace. The low state of religion in this place, and the
corruption of the principle too fully prove such a sad case.

Livermore

Visit David Learned's family, and being unwell, spent the day
with this pleasant and desirous couple. Gave them instruction
and Hemmenway's sermon. She is quite modest and obliging,
and gave me a successful cordial for my cholic. Invited by the
wife of Abijah Munroe, and put up with them for the night.
He had just sprung his net on six dozen pigeons, and took them
all. Grasshoppers were hurtful here, and in several other
places between here and Windham.

Carritunk

Last year the people here were very peaceful, and my preaching right in their esteem, and my company earnestly courted.
I visited them with great hopes that my instructions and books
would put them in a good way of keeping their Sabbaths,
and be of much religious benefit to them. But alas, the disappointment. A part of the people were disciples of Phineas
Randal, the Hopkinsian, and a part, of the Methodists. My
performances were now faulty.

Norridgewogg

Preached all day from three texts; on a dovelike temper as
peculiarly Christian. I believe I was acceptable to most.

The people are nearly divided into two equal bodies—between the Methodists and high Calvinists. Part of the large church of Congregationalists are turned Methodist. They both, I think, go into extremes. Rode to Brother Calef's of Canaan. He is in trouble; his people joining the Baptists under a new idea that he is unconverted. Yet his life is meek, humble, and greatly exemplary; and his preaching, as I believe, scriptural and faithful.

Canaan

Went to Mr. Russell's and got my boots mended.

Sidney

Visited Squire Lovejoy, blind. Heard Mr. Searle, the Methodist. Went home with Mr. Newcomb, grieving at the preaching of Mr. Searle, who, as Mr. Stoneman told me, is a man of learning. I pitied the people, and wished them more capable of distinguishing between God's truth and man's wild fancies. My horse swam over the river forty rods. Preached in the evening at Mr. Taylor's. Mrs. Taylor was enthusiastic and her sister not so. The conversation was a curiosity, and I hope not a useless one.

Vassalboro'

Rode down to Squire Getchel's and preached in the evening. The house was two storied, four rooms painted, a kitchen added, a shed with a room at each end, two barns and a store. His kind wife is a Quaker, and he has been one. We had an excellent supper, and the apple pie tasted like quince or something extra. The Squire lives well, and I was cordially invited to his home, once for all. The Squire has two hundred acres and four hundred in a good farm. Last night a saw mill on the farm was burned down. The Squire bore the loss well. He rode with me to Augusta.

Augusta

Put up and dined with Gideon Lambert, at whose house I had called two years before. Examined the social library which he keeps. Some books are well chosen, others not. Lambert and his wife are ministerial and kind folks, free from new and mad doctrines, Christians in simplicity. She is a good cook, and will smile when you tell her so. They have a good farm, and apples now; but in the first year of our war with England, they lived during the Summer almost without bread.

Windham

Rode to Windham and lodged with Ichabod Hanson, who had eleven children, and never gave one of them a blow, and twenty grandchildren, and never lost one.

Raymondton

Lodged with Lewis Gay. Gay owns much good timber, and hauled logs last winter which sold for six hundred dollars. Rode over the Pond and attended a Baptist Quarterly meeting. The meeting confirmed the sentence of the church of Leech, in excommunicating a Mr. Standish, who secreted, by guile, a child had by his single daughter, Hannah; and against his son for drunkenness. The meeting lasted from 10.0 a.m. till sunset. Services of the Communion which they celebrated, were a prayer—singing—prayer—singing—exhortation—exhortation —prayer, before the reception of the bread and wine. Most of them prayed as if in the greatest distress, and the body of them groaned in time of prayer, and at its end at once ceased. Very little of the knowledge of the word of God and duty appeared.

Norway

Rode to Squire Rust's of Norway. He was absent; his generous wife at home. The weather was very hot and dry.

Hebron

Had much religious conversation with the people of this town. Two Baptist ministers are among them, Hutchinson at the East, and Tripp at the West. The former is ignorant and very earnest and loud, not to say mad. The night meetings held by him are indecent, and an open door to undue freedom among the sexes. Young men invite one another to go to them with such views.

Buckfield

This morning after a rain is pleasant, all things green, and clover fit for mowing. Visited three families yesterday. Mrs. Taylor is ninety years old, was born at Haverhill, and remembers Mrs. Dustin killing seven Indians. Her husband, with one hand only, built more than two hundred mills.

Hartford

Rode to Bartlett's and preached to a pretty good number. Lodged with Freeman Ellis, and was kindly treated by him and his wife, and very kindly by his daughter, deaf, dumb, but very careful, attentive, and industrious. Mrs. Ellis has found poppies and carraway seed very good in helping relaxed bowels, being free from the disorder four years thereby. Visited Major Learned. Mrs. Learned only was at home. She is, in person and behaviour, quite engaging, attentive, decent and industrious.

Livermore

Rode to my friend, Jonathan Morse, the excellent blacksmith. He set anew my horse's fore shoes. Put up with Abijah Munroe for the night. Crossed the ferry and rode four miles in a good road to Squire Solomon Bates of Fayette. Preached in the evening to a serious audience from Acts 17, 30, 31. Lodged with Doctor Hall. Here in Fayette was witchcraft in plenty.

Farmington

Preached from Romans 8, 16, and Luke 16, 26, 31. Rainy morning. It was cloudy, and the audience rather small; attention good and singing sweet. The meek and obliging and industrious Mrs. Sterling was so pleased with my preaching, as, for the first time, to open her heart to me, and conversed like one who wished to maintain a pure heart and blameless life; and to avoid all extremes and angry disputes of doctrines and useless opinions.

Called at Mr. Smith's and conversed with his serious and mild tempered wife; at Mr. Cushman's, and had a friendly and religious visit. Prayed with his feeble wife and mother. Crossed the river and preached at Squire Belcher's; had most excellent singing.

A fine morning after frost. Found Captain Coffin's family well. He gave me most excellent cherry brandy. Rode to Captain Pease's. He was at sea. She is a most affable and sincere woman. She said I was kinder than her own minister who had not visited her. She is bookish, and admirably frank and sociable, and would, I conceive, make a lovely woman, and an excellent Christian under good advantage.

Spoke to Mrs. Backus, a good old lady, wishing for regular ministers, divine ordinances and Sabbaths. She was not pleased with lay teachers and their way of making disciples.

Anson

The famous Ben Randal, too much esteemed here, came to town and deprived me of my lecture. He preached in the forenoon on rebirth. No preaching, however, in the afternoon. Two women prayed and two men exhorted besides Father

Tingley and Randal. It was a miserable and gloomy day. In the evening they had another meeting, in which their restrained zeal had full scope. They could be heard a mile.

Carritunk
The people are divided between the Methodists and the Hopkinsians and are to be pitied.
Rode to Fairfield and dined with friend Bodfish; then back to the settlements and dined with Squire Toby. All friends well, rich and kind.

Fairfield
A beautiful morning. Preached in the new meeting house. Mr. Bodfish had this day a tooth drawn, hoping thereby to help a sore or swelling which seemed to grow from his jawbone. This sore alarmed him and made him more religiously teachable.

Sidney
In the afternoon visited Squire Lovejoy who is blind. He had been a loose liver, of infidel opinions. He once aimed to believe that God would never suffer any man to be forever miserable; and that we die like beasts. He was under painful convictions and inclined to despair. As he once aimed to disbelieve the scriptures, so he now seemed incapable of receiving the comfort of them when he believed. He was much afraid of coming to poverty also. He should be a great warning to men of loose principles and corrupt lives.
Sabbath. Preached at Smiley's. A good number heard with attention. The people here, as in other places visited, are void of schools, and children are neglected, and men cannot write, and some cannot read. Likely young women, dressed as ladies, have vacant minds, which being instructed, would render them very amiable. Polly Tiffany was informed, and wished for further instruction. I hardly saw another of that character.

Winthrop
Rode to Winthrop and lodged at the house of Mr. Metcalf, with the Reverend Belding lately being ordained there. He is esteemed by his people and seems successful. Two or three infidels have been reclaimed. Rode to Mr. Sprague's of Green. The people there are half Baptists, one quarter Methodists, a few Friends, and the rest Congregationalists. Rode through North Gloucester, Gray, and a part of Falmouth, and put up

with Colonel Tyng of Gorham; was tired and not well, but was nursed and recruited.

In summing up his missionary tours through the various parts of Maine, the Reverend Paul Coffin wrote:

The territory of Maine consists of much rich land back from the sea. It is rapid in population, healthy and flourishing. Corn is now one of the most plentiful articles of their produce; and yet it was once thought that the country would in corn especially, fail. It wants, eminently, schools, and pious and learned ministers.

Want of learning, religion, and love of order, suffers the people to be imposed on by quacks in divinity, politics and physic. It is capable of being a happy sojournment. The means of living, are, perhaps, as many, and as productive as can, on the whole be desired. Industry and economy will probably make the inhabitants as rich as is best.

. . . Once delivered from its difficulties on the heads of information and religion, it will bid fair to rise to eminence.

There are, I conceive, fifty or sixty plantations in it capable of ordaining ministers, and gradually supporting them. Religious firmness and integrity in the people would accomplish this most important business, but how much time will be necessary to bring them to this character is hard to determine. The present prejudices against learning in general are strong in many, and divers and strange doctrines are taught and received by thousands.

Chapter 5

'Tre, Pol, and Pen' — The Cornish in Maine.

As a pure-blooded Cor-
nishwoman, I have been
particularly interested in
the fact that early Maine
had quite a Cornish ele-
ment.

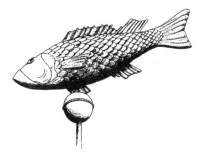

The Cornish people,
though numerically small,
are nonetheless distinctive.
From prehistoric times the Cornish have inhabited the
little peninsula at the extreme South-West end of Britain.
Crude flint tools and other artifacts have been discovered
in Cornwall, dating from about 14,000 years ago. There
are many ancient stone circles in various parts of Cornwall, many of which date from 1800 B.C. It is believed
that some primitive religious ceremony took place there,
with spectators seated on the surrounding bank. Many
gigantic granite tombs are to be found in Cornwall, and
these also date from around 1800 B.C.

Cornwall, unlike the rest of England, has an unbroken
history of some 1500 years of Christianity. The Christianity which came to much of Britain when the Romans invaded, was subsequently suppressed by the heathen
English (Saxons), who also entered Britain from the east.
However, the heathens failed to stamp out Christianity
in the remoter and more mountainous west — Cornwall,
Wales and Ireland — and so it was that until the English
themselves became converted to Christianity after 597
A.D., only this western Celtic fringe remained Christian.

The Roman lawyer, Tertullian, wrote in 208 A.D., 'In
the parts of Britain inaccessible to the Romans, there are
Christians.' It is believed that one of these areas was
Cornwall. From the sixth to the ninth centuries, a great

125

number of missionaries came to Cornwall from Ireland, Brittany andWales. They were anxious to strengthen the Church in Cornwall, and today many of Cornwall's towns bear the names of some of the saints who founded many of her churches; for example, Perranporth (Saint Piran) and St. Ives (Saint Ia), Padstow, anciently known as Petroc-stow (Saint Petroc), St. Mawes, St. Neot, and many others. About four hundred early Christian monuments are to be found in Cornwall, most of them of Cornish granite. One of these, Saint Piran's Cross, near Perranporth, is at least one thousand years old.

John Wesley, the founder of Methodism, first visited Cornwall in 1743, hoping to breathe fresh life into a Church which the Reformation had all but destroyed. With his brother, Charles, and others, he visited Cornwall almost every year until 1789, and spent a great deal of time in the tin mining areas. By the time of Wesley's last journey in 1789, many 'preaching houses' or chapels had been erected, and Methodism had taken a firm hold in the county.

During the late 16th and early 17th centuries, the appearance and the economy of Cornwall were little changed from the Middle Ages. Fish was of vital importance in Cornwall's economy, forming the basic diet of its people, and providing an export trade to the Roman Catholic countries of Europe. Cornwall was noted, too, for its tin and copper mining, and the once famous toast of the Cornish was, 'Fish, tin and copper.'

Surrounded as Cornwall is, almost entirely by water, and with their restricted resources, the Cornish have always been great people for emigrating. Transit by water in the early days was easier than by land, and Scotland, to them, was just another foreign country. Some of the Cornish fishing folk knew the far side of the Atlantic better than London or even Exeter.

Until just over two hundred years ago, Cornwall had its own Celtic language. Today it is spoken only as an acquired language by a few Cornish people, anxious to keep it alive.

There is an old Cornish saying,

> By Tre, Pol, and Pen
> Ye shall know the Cornishmen.

Among names of early settlers in New England can be found the names Treweek, Trescott, Tremayne, Treworgy, Trelawny, Penrose, Pengilly, Penhallow, Pearce, Hocking, Rundle, and many other Cornish names. It is believed that there are hundreds of people in the United States today with the name Chenoweth. The name is a pure Cornish one, meaning 'new house'.

In 1631, one of Sir Ferdinando Gorges' associates was Robert Trelawny, a well-known Plymouth merchant, and son of a famous Cornish family. Trelawny became extremely enthusiastic about the new lands across the Atlantic, and spent a great deal of his fortune in exploration and attempts to form settlements in Maine. In 1635, Trelawny sent out to Maine his younger brother, Edward, from the parish of St. Germans (a few miles from my home in Cornwall) to survey the area and speed settlement there. He sailed with many others from Plymouth and parts of Cornwall. There were Alexander and William Freethy, from the Freethy farm in the village of Saint John (again, just about three miles from my old home in Cornwall); Nicholas Edgcumbe, a poor relation of the great Edgcumbe family; James and John Treworgy, and many others.

The Treworgys, along with one of the Champernoun family, John Edgcumbe, and others, were the founders of Piscataqua, now the towns of Kittery, Eliot, and Berwick. The Treworgys were people of standing in the area, and the name continued. John Treworgy married and had children, and lived at Sturgeon Creek in Kittery, until he went to Newfoundland as Commissioner for the Commonwealth. Among the first settlers of Ellsworth were Mark and Daniel Treworgy. I was delighted, when I arrived in

Orono, to discover a family by the name Treworgy in our church, and to talk with them of their Cornish ancestry.

Captain Richard Bonython, who was baptized at St. Columb Major in Cornwall in 1580, was over fifty when he came with a son and two daughters to Maine. He became joint proprietor, with Thomas Lewis, of the land embracing the present town of Saco, and became a leading member of the little colony there. He became a member of the first court in 1640, and a councillor to the Deputy Governor, Thomas Gorges.

Many Plymouth men were among Maine's first settlers. Nearly one hundred of their names appear in papers relating to the patent of Robert Trelawny. Emigrants were drawn not only from the city of Plymouth, but also from the surrounding villages of Devon and Cornwall. For example, we read of indentures being signed by Trelawny for Paul Mitchell, a sailor from the little parish of Sheviock in Cornwall, and Benjamin Stephens of Landrake, also in Cornwall.

In thirty years from the landing on Plymouth Rock, the New England colonies had taken on a strong West Country flavour; they were largely inhabited by families from Devon and Cornwall, Somerset and Dorset. That flavour has never left Maine and parts of Massachusetts.

Names of Cornish origin spread throughout the New World, the Pearces, the Penhallows, the Treworgys, and so on, and continue to this day.

Robert Trelawny was born at Plymouth on March 25, 1598. His home was at Ham (Weston Ham), in the parish of Pennycross, about two or three miles from the town. Robert was descended from a branch of the ancient and distinguished Trelawny family, which had flourished for a very long time in the county of Cornwall. At the time of the Norman conquest the family was represented by Hamelin de Treloen, who lived at Trelone, in the parish of Alternon in Cornwall. The Trelawny family, then, was one of the most ancient and eminent in the West of England. One of the great Trelawnys was the illustrious knight, Sir John Trelawny, who, in the wars with France, especially at the battle of Agincourt, so greatly distinguished himself, that King Henry V granted him a pension for life, and added to his coat of arms, three oak leaves, the symbol of conquest.

At a later period lived the illustrious prelate, Sir Jonathan Trelawny, Lord Bishop of Bristol. In the year 1688, Sir Jonathan had the courage, with Archbishop Sancroft and five other bishops, to refuse the publication in their churches, of King James II's 'Declaration of Liberty of Conscience,' as it was called. Sir Jonathan Trelawny was committed, with six other bishops, to the Tower of London by the enraged king, and afterwards brought to trial in Westminster Hall, where they were all acquitted and later released, to the great joy of the whole country. In Cornwall, their Bishop's committal to prison and trial angered and stirred up the people of Cornwall, and the following well-known ballad was written and sung throughout the country:

> And shall Trelawny die? and shall Trelawny die?
> Forty thousand Cornishmen will know the reason why.

The father of Robert Trelawny, also Robert, had settled at Plymouth in the reign of Queen Elizabeth, where he became a very successful merchant, and by his ability and integrity, rose so high in the estimation of his fellow townsmen that he was asked to serve as mayor of Plymouth. This Robert Trelawny died in December, 1627, and was interred in a vault in Saint Andrew's church in the centre of Plymouth.

Robert succeeded his father in that year. With his father's estates in Devon and Cornwall, he also inherited his reputation as a successful and enterprising merchant, for it was early in 1630 that he appears to have directed his speculations to the great American continent. Already, the coast of New England was attracting many pioneers from England, and numerous settlements were beginning to occupy the land within the Massachusetts jurisdiction.

As early as 1606, King James I had granted the petition of certain rich merchants and noblemen, including Sir Ferdinando Gorges, exclusive rights to trade and settle the new lands in North America. It was under this patent that Robert Trelawny and Moses Goodyear, merchants of Plymouth, obtained a grant of land in Maine. Trelawny's grant included Richmond Island and all of Cape Elizabeth. This grant was made to Trelawny and Goodyear, who married Gorges' daughter, as a reward for their having expended great sums of money in the discovery of the area, and for their encouragement in settling a plantation there. This patent was signed by the Earl of Warwick, Edward Gorges, and Sir Ferdinando Gorges on 1st of December, 1631. A Mr. John Winter, 'a grave and discreet man,' was appointed by Goodyear and Trelawny as their agent in the new land, and he was placed in possession of the tract by Richard Vines of Saco on 21st of July, 1632.

John Winter, in making his annual returns, and in his numerous letters to Trelawny, shows himself to have been an active and intelligent manager. In a very short time, it appears he was employing almost a fleet of trading vessels, one of them of three hundred tons, and another of six hundred tons, quite sizeable ships in those early days. Their exports consisted principally of pipe-staves, fish, beaver skins and oil, and their imports from the coasts of Spain and Portugal, were wine, fruit, and other products. Trelawny took an immense interest in the success of the trading voyages of these ships. He was far too busy, however, at home, in the management of his domestic affairs and his estates in Devon and Cornwall, to take the time to cross the Atlantic. He was completely confident in John Winter's agency, and so occupied himself fully in his Plymouth counting houses and in civic affairs. Like his father, he, too, became mayor of Plymouth.

Trelawny's loyalty to the throne and his attachment to the Established Church were well known. Indeed, he had made himself so popular with all parties and had gained such a hold on the love and confidence of the people, that even at the critical and eventful period of 1639, he was unanimously chosen by the people of Plymouth to be their representative in Parliament. It must have been obvious to a man of Trelawny's discernment that a mood of sullen discontent towards the throne and the Established Church was growing rapidly among the people. It must, therefore, have been a very courageous action on his part, to leave his quiet and private life and throw himself on the troubled waters of that time. Trelawny was no doubt fully alive to the growing dangers of his position, but was ready, nevertheless, to do his duty in spite of all hazards.

Shortly after Trelawny took his seat in the House of Commons, the struggle had already commenced between the king and his Parliament. This culminated at last, after many conflicts, in open rupture and civil war. In these dangerous days, however moderate a man's opinions might be, and however guarded he might be in expressing them, even in private society, no one was safe. The good and cautious Robert Trelawny did not escape. His well known loyalty to the king and the Established Church soon brought him into trouble. He soon found himself to be a marked man and he was persecuted bitterly. In Lord Clarendon's *History of the Rebellion*, the treatment Trelawny received is described graphically.

In this particular (in oppressing all those who were of different opinions from them), their carriage was so notorious and terrible that spies were set upon, and enquiries made upon all private, light, casual discourses which fell from those who were not gracious to them: Mr. Trelawny of the House of Commons, and a

merchant of great reputation, was expelled from the House and
committed to prison, for having said in a private discourse in the
city to a friend 'that the House could not appoint a guard for
themselves without the king's consent, under pain of high
treason'.

. . . Afterwards, upon the old stock of their dislike, when the
war began to break out, they again imprisoned this honest
gentleman; seized upon all his estate, which was very good, and
suffered him to die in prison for want of ordinary relief and
refreshment.

In this wretched prison, Winchester House, formerly
the palace of the bishops of Winchester, but now converted into a state prison for the Royalists by the Parliament, Robert Trelawny was confined and there died. He
made his last will on 24th of August, 1643, and it is
probable that he died in the early part of 1644. By such an
early death, at the age of forty six, England lost an
enterprising and devoted citizen, and the Church a loyal
and faithful son. The two wills which Trelawny left behind, demonstrate the depth and beauty of his character.
They leave no doubt that a strong religious faith was the
basis of his whole life, a strong desire to serve and benefit
his fellow men. At the very time he was enduring all the
sufferings of imprisonment, the sorrow of his wife's
death, the confiscation of all his estates, and the barbarous withdrawal of 'even ordinary relief and refreshment,' not a word of wrathful indignation or anger
escaped him. He wrote only of himself as 'a prisoner
according to the sadness of the times.' His wills showed
clearly how truly beneficent he had always been, in de-
voting large sums of his money to charitable purposes.

After Trelawny's death, John Winter continued for a
while to carry on the plantation in Maine for Trelawny's
son, John, then only about ten years old. However, after
a time, owing to Winter's death in about 1645, lack of
money, and war between the Indians and settlers, there
was an inevitable and thorough collapse of the Trelawny
venture. The property for which Trelawny had laboured
so hard and spent so much was allowed to pass away

from the family of one of the earliest of Maine's colonists, and all attempt at recovery was impossible.

James Phinney Baxter, in *The Trelawny Papers* (1884), wrote of 'this hasty and unjust decision—unjust because it does not appear that the executors of Robert Trelawny had any time allowed them for appeal.'

In *Western Antiquity, or Devon and Cornwall Note Book*, edited by W. H. K. Wright, F.R.H.S., Librarian for Plymouth, is found this further information on Trelawny:

Some time in the year 1872, John Wingate Thornton of Boston, Massachusetts was looking at an English catalogue. He noticed an advertisement, inserted by a London bookseller regarding an old document which was said to bear the signature of Robert Trelawny.

In 1631, Robert, a successful merchant in Plymouth, England, obtained a grant of land in Maine, including Richmond's Island and Cape Elizabeth, from 'the Council established at Plymouth, in the county of Devon, for the planting, governing, etc. of New England in America.'

The original patent, according to Willis, the historian, of Portland, had been destroyed by the wife of a descendant of Robert Jordan, 'needing some paper to keep her pastry from burning, she had taken from a chest of papers, Trelawny's patent, & used it for that purpose, which thus perished, like many other ancient and valuable manuscripts.'

Mr. Thornton, an indefatigable antiquarian, at once wrote to the London bookseller, asking him to forward the document, but was informed that it had been sold to Rev. C. T. Collins Trelawny, of Ham, near Plymouth, a descendant of Robert Trelawny.

Mr. Thornton opened a correspondence with Rev. C. T. Collins Trelawny, in the course of which he was told that in the old house at Ham, still owned by the Trelawny family, was a chest containing many old papers. A list of these papers was sent to Thornton, who found they comprised a voluminous correspondence between Trelawny and John Winter, the 'Governor' of Trelawny's plantation in Maine, and the original patent. There were, too, valuable letters from others, throwing new light upon the early history of Maine.

These important papers were presented to the Maine Historical Society by the Rev. C. T. Collins Trelawny. But for Thornton's perseverance in following up an old document of uncertain value, advertised by a London bookseller, these papers, which had lain in the old house at Ham, Plymouth, for nearly 250 years, might never have seen the light.

Now, more than three hundred years after his death, I, a Cornishwoman, not content to let Trelawny pass unrecognized in Maine, adapt the old verse to read:

> And shall Trelawny die?
> Here's just one Cornishwoman
> Shall know the reason why.

Chapter 6

From Log Cabin to Frame House.

The morning of July 4th, 1976 was perfect in every way — not too hot, not too cool, with a clear blue cloudless sky. It was a special day — the 200th Anniversary of the signing of the Declaration of Independence, and it was going to be celebrated in a special way in Orono. The Main Street was closed to traffic,  and in front of our beautiful, white, wooden church the road was filled with one thousand chairs. By ten o'clock all these chairs were filled, and a choir of two hundred, many of them wearing Colonial dress, were arranged on the grassy area in front of the church. It was an awe-inspiring occasion, and the three ministers of the town, the genial Catholic priest, the tall and pleasant Methodist minister, and my husband, the English minister of the Community church, made it a real and meaningful Ecumenical service. It was truly a day to remember, and we felt grateful to be there and to be part of it. When the other ministers had generously suggested that my husband should preach the sermon, he smilingly declined, saying that perhaps on this particular occasion it should be an American.

There had been great celebrations all the previous week, with all kinds of activities, such as fireworks, a chicken barbecue, a baked bean supper, canoe races on the river, a costume ball with everyone in Colonial dress, an antique show, a horse show and a huge Parade. The

Parade was great fun, with clowns, bands, floats, horses with riders in Indian dress, and so on. The girls of the Millinocket Pink Panthers band marched past playing with great precision and expertise, their tan and shocking-pink uniforms making a dazzling addition to the already colourful scene. All in all it was a really enjoyable time for everyone.

It struck me over this time how little I really knew of American history. The Bicentennial had stimulated my interest and made me determined to at least learn more of the history of Maine, the life of the people in the early days, and some of the interesting characters whose lives had made an impact on the State.

Centuries before the Europeans crossed the ocean to the shores of North America, it is believed that a race known today as the Red Paint People lived here. These aborigines, it is believed, lived about five thousand years ago. Some of the leading anthropologists feel the Red Paint People may have been of Eskimo origin, while others think they were the ancestors of Maine's Indians. No one really knows for certain. Great heaps of shells found on the Maine coast dating from one thousand to five thousand years ago indicate that shellfish must have constituted part of their diet.

It is probable that the coast of Maine was the first part of America to be seen by the early explorers. It is said that about five hundred years before Columbus crossed the Atlantic, Leif Ericson, the son of Eric the Red, left Norway for Greenland with a crew of thirty oarsmen. They lost their way in a bad storm and fog, and reached a coast which they had never seen before, and which was unnamed. This is believed to have been the coast of Maine. A Norse coin dated 1000 A.D., found recently in the Blue Hill area of Maine, seems to make this claim of Norse discovery much more likely.

When Christopher Columbus, a Genoese navigator in the service of Spain, returned in 1493 with his reports of a new land and the strange people who inhabited it, there was great excitement in the whole of Europe. In France, Italy, Holland and England, in the castles of the noblemen, in the homes of rich merchants, and even among the seamen in the taverns, his discovery was the chief topic of conversation. King Henry VII of England became intensely interested in this new land across the ocean, and in 1497 sent a Venetian seaman, John Cabot, with his son Sebastian in ships fitted out by merchants of Bristol. The Cabots discovered Newfoundland, Nova Scotia, and the coast of Maine, and it was upon this voyage that England based most of its later claims to the New World. The French, too, were interested in this exciting new land, and in 1524 they employed Giovanni de Verrazano, an Italian explorer, to lead an expedition. He, too, returned with glowing reports of fine forests and vast quantities of fish to be found there.

As the 1500's passed, other explorers and adventurous fishermen sailed along the Maine coast and returned with the holds of their ships filled with valuable dried cod. However, settlements in this area were not attempted until the early 1600's when France based her claims to North America on the explorations of Verrazano, and England on the discoveries of Cabot. In the struggle for supremacy which followed, the Maine settlers were in a difficult position between the English power in Massachusetts, and the French power in Acadia (now the Provinces of Nova Scotia, New Brunswick, and Prince Edward Island, parts of Quebec and Maine) which they claimed.

Acceding to the throne of England in 1558, Elizabeth I was proud of the Navy which her father, Henry VIII, had built, and encouraged merchants, traders, and 'sea dogs' to take voyages and seek new wealth for her realm. She was determined to make England the world's leading power. Some of the great Elizabethan 'sea dogs' included Sir Walter Raleigh, Sir Francis Drake, Sir Humphrey Gilbert and Sir John Hawkins. There were many great sea battles in the struggle for supremacy, and in 1588 the Spanish Armada was defeated, leaving England as the undisputed ruler of the seas. The way was now open for the English to consider the possibility of colonizing in the New World across the seas. This was to be the beginning of the greatest colonial empire of modern times, with possessions on every continent.

On the death of Elizabeth in 1603, King James I acceded to the throne. In 1606 a group of noblemen and rich merchants who had become enthused with the spirit of colonization, secured a charter from the king for the purpose of making settlements and carrying on trade in the New World. Since most of the leading men lived in or near the city of Plymouth, they became known as the Plymouth Company. Sir Ferdinando Gorges and Sir John Popham were among the leaders of this Company, and, as we know, from that time until his death in 1647 Gorges was to devote his whole life, his entire energies and fortune to the development of the area which is now the State of Maine.

At about the same time, a French aristocrat, Pierre du Gast, Sieur de Monts, had received trading rights from his government to a vast area of the North American coast. Thus the struggle between France and England for this new territory began.

The people who left their homes and their established, familiar surroundings to settle in a strange land thousands of miles across the ocean, to face an unknown and hazardous future, must have possessed qualities of great courage and determination. The sea voyage was long, the boats were crowded and uncomfortable. Below decks there was little room to move around, and the air was stifling. There was a great deal of sickness, and scurvy was rife. The colonists were relieved to see land after the gruelling journey, and the cold, clean air and the scent of the great pine trees was intoxicating after the unhealthy conditions on the boat. However, the enormous dark forests with their strange wild animals and other unknown dangers were intimidating, so the men set to work at once building homes and stockades. The forests were among the most valuable resources of the new homeland. The settlers needed wood for their homes, for fencing, their tools, their furniture, dishes, and most other household utensils, and it was their only fuel with which to combat the long, hard Winters.

When a suitable place was found, a clearing was made and the building commenced. At first the colonists used huge handsaws: a cut log was placed over a large open pit on a cross timber, and two sawyers manned the saw, one standing in the pit and the other on the cross timber. This was a back-breaking task, however, and in the early towns sawmills were among the first public structures to be built. The first cabins were simple, one room, log structures with sometimes a loft above. The chinks between the logs were filled with moss and clay, and a thatched roof of twigs, straw, or whatever materials were at hand, was put on. The chimneys were of rough stones on the outside wall at the end of the house, and the fireplaces were enormously wide and high. Two or three openings were left for the doors and windows. Sometimes the windows might be protected by a heavy wooden shutter, or rough frames might be attached to the squared ends of the timbers and filled with translucent oiled paper. A heavy plank door was attached by long wooden hinges, some wooden pins driven into the inside wall, on which clothing could be hung, and the cabin was ready for occupation. The furniture was simple, constructed from logs, and held together by wooden pegs. These houses, though somewhat rough and basic, were warm and comfortable, and served the early settlers' purposes until facilities for preparing better building materials were available. In the average household most of the dishes and utensils were made of wood which the men whittled with their knives. Mattresses were filled with straw, or sometimes with feathers plucked from the unlimited supplies of wild geese and ducks.

The men and boys cultivated the fields, raised and harvested the crops, hunted and fished. They cared for and sheared the sheep, made furniture and utensils for the house, and wooden rakes, hoes, and other kinds of implements. Skins of animals were tanned by soaking them in large tubs, then dried, cleaned and rubbed smooth and made into leather. The father had, in the early days, to make shoes for the family. Later, a travelling shoemaker, or cobbler, carried his tools with him as he travelled from farm to farm, making shoes for the family, or mending old ones.

English barnyard animals such as pigs, chickens and goats appear to have been plentiful soon after the arrival of the Pilgrims. The first cattle arrived a little later, and then horses and sheep. After this, most ships bringing emigrants carried livestock. Shipments of goats were especially numerous in the early years. They were hardy animals, less likely to die in transit than most; they took less space than cattle and supplied milk during the voyage. The ships carrying new settlers also carried cargoes placed on board by enterprising merchants, or even by the ships' captains themselves.

The pioneer women and girls worked as hard as the men and boys. They made candles of tallow from the bodies of animals, or from bayberries gathered by the children. The candles were made by dipping wicks of loosely spun cord into a cauldron of melted tallow. The candles had to be dipped again and again until they reached the required thickness; they were then hung on racks to harden. Hundreds of candles were needed to light a house during the long Maine Winters, so there had to be a large supply. Many of the settlers had brought spinning wheels and looms with them, and the women and girls did all the spinning and weaving in order to provide clothing for the family. The wool was first carefully washed, then combed out to make it light and fluffy. Next, it was dyed in great iron pots in colouring matter obtained from herbs, bark, berries and roots. It was then spun and woven into cloth. The clothing of the pioneer family was made from materials of the most durable quality. Men wore leather breeches made from the skins of deer, sheep and calves. The women's dresses were plain and simple, but the homespun material was substantial and warm, and would wear and wear until the owner became tired of them. A new dress in the early pioneer days was a great occasion indeed.

The women had to learn how to cut up the bodies of animals, and to salt and pickle them for storage for the winter. They learned how to cook new foods such as corn bread, baked beans, pumpkin pies. Each family had to depend upon itself entirely for food supplies. They raised sheep, and guarded them zealously against wolves and other predators. The forests abounded in deer, bears, moose and other animals. Wild geese, ducks, and turkeys flocked everywhere. The rivers teemed with salmon and other fish which were caught in such quantities with trap, spear and hook, that barrels of them were cured and kept for winter use. Every conceivable kind of wild berry grew in great abundance, and these were picked and made into pies, jams and preserves, or sweetened with maple syrup and eaten as they were. In the spring the men bored holes in the trunks of the sugar maple trees and put spouts into them, then buckets were hung under the spouts to catch the running sap. Big fires were built and the sap was boiled into clear, sweet maple syrup. Soft soap was obtained by boiling down fat with lye made from wood ashes.

Doctors were few and far between in the early settlements, and were seldom available to the pioneers.

The women became the only doctors for their families. They learned to set broken bones, to clean and bind up wounds, to assist in childbirth, and to 'lay out' the bodies of their dead. They cultivated herbs such as camomile, tansy, sage, dock, catnip, peppermint, spearmint, wormwood and poppies, and gathered roots, wild herbs and berries from the woodlands and fields. They stored away ragweed, burdock, plantain, sumac and elderberries, and from these, simple medicinal herbs, teas, syrups, and healing salves were made by boiling and simmering. These were then administered to any member of the family who had a chill or cold, a wound which needed healing, or any other common ailment.

The children became independent at a very early age. They picked berries for cooking and preserving, bayberries for candle-making, helped the mother prepare food, and looked after the younger children. The inhabitants of the early settlements were dependent upon each other, for companionship, for help and support, perhaps for very existence. They would assist each other to build homes and barns, and in times of illness, trouble, or danger, were generous and thoughtful. If a neighbour had killed a sheep or cow, a generous piece of the meat was given to a nearby family, or when a man had been fishing and came home with a good catch of trout or other fish, he invariably divided it with his neighbours.

Once the homes were built, one of the first buildings to be erected in any new settlement was the church or meeting house. This was a plain wooden building, very bare and without any kind of ornamentation. In the winter the meeting house was cold and uncomfortable. The minister's sermon was usually very long, and in some churches a man kept people awake during the long service by walking up and down the aisles carrying a long rod. Feathers were attached to one end and a knob at the other. If someone started to doze off he was tickled with the feathers in order to rouse him, but if he actually fell asleep he was prodded with the knob. Everyone was expected to attend the church, and illness was the only excuse for staying at home. The men and boys usually sat on one side of the church and the women and girls on the other. People also gathered there for public meetings, for weddings and for funerals. A musket or long rifle were everyday companions to the settler. They hung on buck horns over the fireplaces, stood within reach in the corner of each cabin, were carried to the cornfields and even to church.

Most of the settlers were deeply religious, and at that time the ministers were the most important people in the community. A Reverend Robert Jordan, born in England in 1601, settled on Richmond's Island, Maine, as early as 1640. The Colonial authorities summoned him to Court in 1657, where he was charged with baptizing children and practising the rites of the Church of England contrary to law. This was an example of the religious bigotry possessed by some of those who fled to America to enjoy liberty of conscience, and in turn became persecutors. The beautifully ornamented brass baptismal font used by Jordan has been handed down by his descendants, and is now housed at the Maine Historical Society building in Portland. Another minister in the area in 1685 was paid his salary in beef, pork, wheat, corn, butter, boards and oakstaves.

At first the Indians showed the colonists great friendship, and helped and instructed them in various ways. They taught them snow-shoeing, canoeing and woodcraft. They showed them how to grow corn, beans and squash, and traded with the settlers, bringing them furs in exchange for cloth and domestic utensils. Gradually this friendliness began to disappear, as the Indians became aware that they were fast losing their lands and hunting grounds. The first real war came when an Indian chief from Massachusetts, known to the English as King Philip, attacked the settlements there. King Philip's Indian name was Metacomet, and he was the son of Massasoit, the chief who had given great assistance and friendship to the Plymouth Colony. Massasoit had had great influence over all the chieftains of Massachusetts, and for forty five years the Indians were at peace with the settlers. In 1621 the leaders of the Plymouth Colony had assembled to discuss various matters when an Indian was seen approaching. This was Massasoit, who welcomed the colonists warmly and assured them of his friendship. He kept his word, and his tribe remained at peace with the white men until his death.

Metacomet (King Philip) became chief of the Wampanoag tribe in 1662. He was twenty three years old, tall, strong and handsome, with a proud spirit. He pledged himself at first to use every effort to continue the peace which had always existed between his own race and the colonists, and for several years there was peace. Then in 1671 Philip complained bitterly of the encroachment of the English upon his hunting grounds. The settlers had become more demanding. Now clearings and farms began to spoil the huge trackless forests where the Indians could once roam at will. Now they were being forbidden to hunt and fish in the streams near by, and the once silent forests echoed with the sounds of the axe and saw, and falling trees. The Indian chief began to reflect upon the future when all his hunting grounds would vanish, and the Indians would be driven out completely as more and more settlers arrived. The war in Massachusetts started on June 20th, 1675, and spread rapidly to Maine when King Philip sent messengers asking his brothers there to join him in the struggle to retain their lands. The Abenakis of Maine began to attack the small settlements and lonely farmhouses. Homes were burned and many of the settlers were killed. The settlements in Maine were small and scattered so that they were extremely vulnerable to attack. The settlers soon realized they must build some sort of fortification in order to protect their families from constant attack.

They appealed to the General Court in Boston for funds to erect garrison houses. These were simple stockades of hewn timber entrenched in the ground, and inside this a strong building called a blockhouse. These blockhouses were constructed so that they could be defended from all directions. The second storey extended beyond the first and had holes in the floor so that the defenders inside could fire down upon any Indian who tried to get close enough to set fire to the building. They could fire through loopholes in the projecting floor without exposing themselves at the windows. Sentinels were kept constantly on the watch, and men were armed at all times. Nothing could prevent the Indians from sniping, however, and their stealthy methods of ambush warfare gave them the advantage. When an alarm was given by the firing of a gun, everyone ran for the garrison or fort, and sometimes they were forced to remain there for a considerable time, herded together in close quarters, with scanty food supplies and lack of air.

After King Philip was killed in 1676 both settlers and Indians, exhausted by over a year of cruel warfare, were eager for peace. A treaty was signed, and for about a decade life went on normally and peacefully. In the meantime the French had been very active in establishing a thriving colony at Port Royal in Nova Scotia. They had gained the confidence of the Indians in that area, and had succeeded in laying the foundation of a permanent and profitable business with them. France was claiming, too, territory which the English felt rightfully belonged to them by reason of their discovery. England and France had been rivals in Europe for a very long time, and in 1689 war broke out between the two countries. This of course meant that the subjects of these countries now settled in North America, also became involved in the struggle.

About this time three outstanding men, very different in character and background, emerged. They were all

born in the 1650's, and each would become involved in
Maine's history. The first of these was William Phips.
William was born in a rough cabin on the bank of a river,
in the town of Woolwich in the Kennebec region in 1651.
He was one of more than twenty children born to James
and Mary Phips, who first came to the area in 1638. As
she looked down at this latest addition to her already
large family, Mary Phips could not know then that this
boy would one day become Governor of New England,
would be knighted by the king of England, would discover
valuable sunken treasure in the Bahamas, and would
help to save Maine from French and Indian domination.

As a boy William worked on the land, tending the
sheep, cutting wood, and growing crops. He was a strong,
tough boy, fearless, self-reliant, and above all, ambitious.
At the age of eighteen he decided he wanted more out of
life than this and left home. He made his way by canoe to
a place called Arrowsic, where he apprenticed himself
for four years as a shipwright. During those years William
became filled with the great desire to see foreign lands,
and to seek his fortune. At the end of the apprenticeship
he worked his way to Boston and got a job in a shipyard.
Living in Boston made him realise how little he knew,
and he made up his mind to learn to read and write.
This he achieved very quickly, and became even more
ambitious. He promised himself that one day he would
captain his own ship, and would own a brick house in a
wealthy part of Boston.

While William was in Boston he met the widow of a
Captain John Hull, and later married her. Now that he
had influential and wealthy connections Phips soon
managed to secure a contract to build a ship, and re-
membering the vast forests of his native Maine returned
to his old home and began to work on his ship. At last the
ship was ready, and on a day in August, 1676, lay at
anchor, loaded with timber to be taken to Boston. An
Indian raiding party descended on the area just as Phips

was about to set sail. The terrified inhabitants, including his own family, appealed to William for help. He responded immediately by throwing the timber overboard, piling the refugees aboard his ship, and setting sail for Boston and safety. This daring feat gave William the reputation for resourcefulness and courage, and he became something of a hero. Soon after this he became captain of a ship engaged in trade in the West Indies. While he was there Phips constantly heard tales of sunken Spanish galleons, their holds filled with gold, jewels, and other treasures, and he determined that somehow he must recover this vast wealth. He sailed to England to persuade King Charles II to support this venture, and after months of patient waiting he eventually gained an audience with the king. Charles was interested to hear about the great riches which might be added to his coffers, and assigned a frigate and one hundred tough seamen to the recovery of the Spanish gold.

After a long, unsuccessful search, the crew became frustrated and angry, and mutinied. William subdued them by sheer force of will and drastic measures. He was compelled to abandon the search and return to England, but inspired such confidence in the eventual success of the enterprise that the Duke of Albemarle and other noblemen fitted out two other ships and dispatched Phips again on his adventurous mission. This time the venture was successful, and William returned to England laden with gold, silver and priceless jewels. He was received with great acclaim, and King James II, who was now on the throne, rewarded Phips' remarkable achievement by knighting him, giving him a commission in the Royal navy, a generous share of the treasure, and a golden cup. The recovery of this valuable treasure was the talk of London, and the man responsible for it was feted and honoured. However, Sir William was eager to return to Boston, to set about building the fine brick house he had promised himself he would one day own. In 1689 he became High Sheriff of Massachusetts, in the same year that war had been declared between France and England. A year later Phips was sent by the Massachusetts government to subdue Nova Scotia, and to capture Port Royal, the French stronghold there. Port Royal was suspected by the Massachusetts Government of outfitting and paying Indian raiders to harass the English settlements, and the authorities in Boston were determined that this headquarters of the French must be captured and put out of action, and that Sir William Phips was just the man to do this. In April, 1690, therefore, he set out with a fleet of ships and a sizeable army. The expedition was successful, and Port Royal surrendered without too much resistance. The English took formal possession of all the coast from the Penobscot River to Port Royal.

The Government, elated by the success, determined to proceed next against Quebec, and Phips, the hero of the previous expedition, was chosen for the command. Thirty two vessels were fitted out and manned with two thousand men. However, this time the venture was not so successful, and the army was forced to retreat. Sir William was appointed Governor of the Province of Massachusetts in 1692. This, of course, included Maine, and the new Governor was particularly interested in the Province in which he was born and which he had lived in until his young manhood. He had a strong garrison built for the protection of Pemaquid, an important trading post with about eight hundred inhabitants. This was Fort William Henry, the largest fortress to be built in Maine at this time, with walls twenty two feet high and eight feet thick.

Phips made enemies, however. Some resented his wealth and fame, and others accused him of maladministration. In 1694 he sailed to England to answer charges against him. He became ill while the case was pending and subsequently died at the early age of forty

three years. He was buried in London — a long way from
the log cabin on the Maine coast where he was born.

Because of the struggle taking place in Europe between
France and England for colonial and maritime supremacy,
the poor pioneers in the disputed territory in this part of
North America were terrorized and killed, their homes
burned, and settlements destroyed. These settlers lived
in constant fear of an attack at any hour of the day or
night. They were surprised continually by blood-curdling
war whoops and flying arrows. The French helped and
encouraged the Indians to drive the English colonists
from New England and, in so doing, naturally furthered
their own ends. Maine colonists were plunged into a long
period of warfare, broken only by intervals of uneasy
truce.

Another man whose life and actions were to have an
impact on the settlements and their inhabitants over
this turbulent period was the colourful, dynamic Baron
de Castin. Jean Vincent, Baron de St. Castin, was born
in 1652, in the district of Bearn, at the foot of the Pyre-
nees. His family owned vast estates there and were
extremely wealthy. When he was fifteen years old, Jean
Vincent joined a famous French regiment, the Carnignan
Salieres. King Louis XIV sent the regiment to fight the
Turks, and the young Castin served with distinction.
The regiment was then sent to Quebec to protect the
French settlements there against the Iroquois Indians,
and after a while was disbanded. Instead of returning to
Bearn where he was heir to the family estates and for-
tune, Castin preferred to remain in what was then known
as New France. While he was at Quebec he met the great
Penobscot chief, Madockawando, when he came to
Montreal and Quebec with great quantities of furs, and
it is likely that Madockawando was largely responsible
for Castin's decision to go to Pentagoet (now Castine,
Maine). At Pentagoet he built a large house and established a trading post. The Indians there soon grew to love

and respect Castin, and regarded him as their protector, almost as some sort of god. Castin learned to speak the Abenaki language fluently and adopted the dress of the Indians. So successful was his trading post that he gradually amassed a considerable fortune, trading with both French and English. The French Government held him in high esteem because of the great influence he exercised over the Indians.

Castin had earned the reputation for loose living, and of having several Indian wives. Monsieur de Menneval, upon becoming Governor of the French province, urged Castin to regulate his way of life, and it seems as though he did listen to this advice, for in 1687 he was legally married to the daughter of Madockawando, named Mathilde. Monsieur de Menneval wrote on the first of December, 1687, 'The Sieur de Castin is absolute master of the savages and of all their business, being in the forest with them, and having with him two of the daughters of the chief of the savages by whom he has many children.' Later, on the tenth of September, 1688, Menneval reported, 'I have induced the Sieur de Castin to live a more regular life. He has quitted his traffic with the English, his debauchery with the savages; he is married, and has promised me to labour to build a settlement in this country.'

During the entire time he lived there, Castin held Pentagoet almost alone as a semi-military trading post. He was a man of great charm and magnetism. The Indians idolized him, but the English wished to uproot this man whom they were beginning to regard as a dangerous neighbour. Early in 1688, Sir Edmund Andros, Governor of New England, made an attempt to seize the fortress at Pentagoet. He sailed in a well equipped frigate and anchored in the harbour directly opposite the fort. Castin and his family went into hiding. Andros landed and pillaged the place, leaving only the altar in the chapel unscathed. He left a message for Castin stating that if he wanted his property returned, he must go to Pemaquid, the English settlement, and acknowledge allegiance to the king of England. Castin was incensed and refused, and it was this act of Andros which was responsible for the ill-will of Castin and his Indian friends towards the English from then on.

On his return to Boston, Andros found that there had been Indian uprisings in Maine, and these were due, it was believed, to Castin's deep resentment of Andros' pillaging of his home. After a time, Chief Madockawando, Castin's father-in-law, visited Boston, accompanied by several sachems, in an endeavour to secure peace. He said that Castin was deeply offended by the unprovoked attack upon his home and the plunder of his property. The French, he said, regarded it as a national insult and a proclamation of war. The Indians, who had adopted Castin into their tribe and made him a chief, considered it no less an act of hostility against them, and thus a terrible war would rage unless terms of peace could be agreed upon. The Government treated the Indians courteously, and assured them of their disapproval of Andros' conduct. They told Madockawando that Andros had been dismissed from office, loaded the chiefs with gifts, and sent, too, a conciliatory letter to Castin. However, by 1689 England and France were at war, and this had great repercussions on the people of Maine. The patriotic pride and the religious fanaticism of the French in Canada were aroused, and they vowed to drive the heretical English out of Maine. The French and Indians fought together, and the effects upon the English colonists were devastating. The French military expertise combined with the cunning of the Indians rendered the situation so dangerous that the settlers hardly knew how to combat the situation. Town after town was destroyed, the buildings reduced to ashes, and large numbers of the inhabitants were either massacred or carried off into captivity.

Fort William Henry was the strongest and most expensive fortification built by the English during William Phips' Governorship. This was at Pemaquid in Maine. Not long after the fortress was completed, a large, well-armed body of Indians and French, led by Castin and others, attacked it. The defenders soon realised how greatly outnumbered they were, and surrendered with very little resistance. By the capture of Fort William Henry the French removed one of the greatest obstacles to their possession of the territory which they claimed between the Penobscot and the Kennebec Rivers in Maine.

Nothing certain is known of Castin's last years. It is believed, however, that around the 1700's he went back to France, and that he died there in 1708. His son, Anselm, who became known as Castin the younger, had inherited his father's courage and charm, as well as the outstanding qualities of his mother's race. He was a man of intelligence and culture, and was the most zealous of all the chieftains in urging peace. He went among the tribes trying to persuade them to lay down their arms. Unfortunately the English mistakenly thought he was trying to incite the Indians, and captured him. He was taken in chains to Boston and kept prisoner there for seven months. Eventually the young Castin succeeded in convincing the authorities that his intention in addressing the tribes had been peaceable, and he was released. He returned to the Abenaki Indians and managed to placate them, and a long period of peace followed.

Maine historian William D. Williamson paid a well-merited tribute to the memory of Castin the Younger. He wrote, 'He appeared to be entirely free from the bigoted malevolence of the French, and the barbarous, revengeful spirit of the savages. He was a chief sagamore of the Tarratine tribe; and he also held a commission from the French king. By his sweetness of temper, magnanimity, and other valuable properties, he was held in high estimation by both people. Nor were the English insensible of his uncommon merit. He had an elegant French uniform which he sometimes wore; yet, on all occasions he preferred to appear in the habit of his tribe. It was in him both policy and pleasure to promote peace with the English.'

The warfare had been devastating to both Indians and English. The starving tribes had longed for peace. Disease and famine had raged among them, and were responsible for the death of Madockawando. English and Indians alike froze and died from exposure and lack of food. There was desolation everywhere, with wrecked cabins, and clearings overgrown. The remaining colonists mourned, as dead, relatives who had been taken by the Indians to Canada. One third of the Indians had perished, and apart from the warriors who had been killed, their wives and children died in conditions of great deprivation. The Indians must have remembered the words of Passaconaway, an old and wise sachem. Before the wars started he had told them, 'Hearken to the last words of your father and friend. The white men are sons of the morning. The Great Spirit is their father. His sun shines bright around them. Never make war with them. Sure as you light the fires, the breath of heaven will turn the flames upon you and destroy you. Listen to my advice. It is the last that I shall be allowed to give you. Remember it and live.'

In the longed-for period of peace which followed, and in spite of the conflicts which had absorbed for so long their strength and energies, there was a period of rapid growth in all directions in Maine. In a remarkably short time the older towns resumed much of their former prosperity, and new settlements began to spring up. Forts and garrison houses were erected in considerable numbers, and everything indicated the determination of the colonists to make their stay permanent. This began to cause great unrest again among the Indians as they saw more and more settlers arrive, farms being cleared, and more encroachment upon their hunting grounds. All these activities were regarded with suspicion and anxiety, and the prospect of being forced gradually to give up possession of all they held most dear filled them with great apprehension.

France's most valuable agents in her struggle for supremacy in the New World were the Jesuit missionaries. Through the dedication and selflessness of these men the Indians were converted in large numbers, and were held by these religious ties to an alliance with the French. Missionary work had been more successful among the Abenaki nation than any other. Unfortunately these mission Indians were destined to become the terror of the New England border. In the letters of Denonville, Governor of New France at the time, there is strong evidence of the part played by the Jesuit priests in the attacks upon the English settlements.

Gabriel Dreuillettes was the first missionary to settle on the banks of the Kennebec River. In 1646 he built a chapel at Old Point, Norridgewock, and taught the Indians there for many years. He was a highly educated and eloquent man, and the Indians held him in high regard. Dreuillettes was succeeded in the mission at Norridgewock by two brothers. They were Vincent and Jacques Bigot, sons of a French baron. These young men from a wealthy home gave up all the attractions of a cultured society, a comfortable life-style, and ambitious aspirations, to spend their lives in a strange, wild land, among a strange, wild people, to teach them Christian truths. Sebastian Rasle succeeded the Bigots in the mission. He, too, was a man with a background of culture and wealth, and religious zeal inspired him, too, to leave a luxurious way of life to go and spend thirty five years in the wilderness of Maine.

Sebastian Rasle was born in France in 1657. He came from an illustrious French family, and trained for the priesthood at the Jesuit College at Lyons. In 1689 he left

France to serve as a missionary in what was then New France. He was thirty two years old at this time, and at first he preached to the Illinois and Huron Indians in Canada. He was then sent to the Abenaki village at Norridgewock on the Kennebec River. Norridgewock was an ideal site for a village. The land was rich and productive, the river teemed with fish, and the forests were filled with deer and other game.

The English viewed the coming of this new Jesuit missionary with some apprehension. Their anxiety was somewhat justified in view of the actions of some of the other priests whom they had had good reason to mistrust. They were convinced that the Jesuits were instrumental in keeping alive the antagonism of the Indians against them. Father Rasle became completely involved in the needs and interests, the joys and sorrows of the Indians. He lived with his flock as their devoted pastor, teacher, doctor, counsellor and friend, and won the love of the whole tribe to an extraordinary degree. His mission became one of the most important Jesuit outposts. By the time Father Rasle arrived on the Kennebec he had already mastered several Indian dialects, and was fluent in the language, so that he was able to understand his people's problems readily and could help them. With his followers he built a church of rough hewn timber surmounted by a cross. Inside, the walls were hung with pictures depicting the Crucifixion and other Biblical scenes. There was silver plate for sacramental services, and as he was a skilful wood-worker, Father Rasle carved ornaments for the beautifying of the church. He accompanied his people when they went to the coast for their annual fishing and the hunting of ducks and sea birds of various kinds. The Indians built a little bark-covered church on an island, and near it a little cabin for the priest. He always carried some of his vestments with him, and the services were performed there just as they were at their village at Norridgewock.

Shortly before his death, in letters to a brother and a nephew, Father Rasle described his mission at Norridgewock and his life there. He painted in these letters a vivid picture of his Indian people, of his love and devotion to them over a period of some thirty years, and the loneliness and sacrifice of his Spartan existence. He wrote that two other missionaries also worked among the Abenakis, but that they were too far away for him to ever see them, and that they saw, heard, and spoke only to Indians. He described the group of about forty young Indian braves he had organized into a group of assistants. They took part in the services, wearing their cassocks and surplices. Each of them had his duties, some helped at Mass, others chanted psalms and took part in the processions on holy days. The women vied with each other in the decoration of the church, and used their jewellery, pieces of silk, and other possessions to make it even more beautiful. The church was brilliantly lit with numerous candles, of which there was always an ample supply. These were ingeniously made from the berries of the bayberry or the wild laurel. The berries were boiled in a pot of water, and when the water boiled the wax rose to the surface and was removed. About four pounds of wax was obtained from three bushels of berries. The wax was pure and good, but not very soft or manageable. To make it pliable, beef, mutton, or moose tallow was added, and this made good, hard, serviceable candles. About two hundred candles more than a foot in length could be made from twenty four pounds of wax, and the same amount of tallow.

The Indians, summoned by a bell, attended the church regularly, in the morning for Mass and for evening prayers at sunset. Father Rasle had composed suitable prayers to enable the Indians to enter into the services fully. These they chanted or recited in loud voices during Mass. After Mass, Father Rasle taught the catechism to the children and young people. The rest of the morning he spent counselling his people on marital problems, complaints against other members of the tribe, and other anxieties. Some he had to instruct, others needed consoling. He re-established peace in families, calmed troubled consciences, and gently corrected others. The afternoons he spent visiting the sick, and going to the cabins of those who needed special instruction. The Indians would make no decisions without Rasle being present at their councils, which they held frequently, and they always accepted his advice. He was invited to all their feasts, and gave the benediction on the food before it was served.

At the beginning of his work at Norridgewock, the Indians allowed Father Rasle very little time of his own for meditation, or even at night to rest. He gradually made them understand that he was not to be disturbed after the evening prayers until Mass the next morning, unless it was for something crucial, such as to assist a dying person, or anything equally important. He was glad of the time on his own, and used it to pray, and to rest from the day's labours. His food was very simple. As he could not adapt to the smoked meat and fish which the Indians ate, his main nourishment was a kind of pudding which he cooked from ground maize and water. This was sweetened with a little syrup. The women collected the sap from the maple trees in the spring in bark dishes, and boiled it to obtain good syrup.

In his letters Father Rasle described the great affection the Indians had for their children. As soon as a baby was born, it was placed on a piece of board covered with cloth. This was the babies' cradle, and they were wrapped in a little bear skin, and carried around on their mothers' backs. The children were taught to draw the bow almost as soon as they could walk, and became so adroit at this that at the age of ten or twelve years they could shoot at and kill a bird. Men, women, and children loved tobacco, and would smoke almost continually. A gift of tobacco would please them more than anything else.

When a chief died, the Indians prepared a vast coffin, and clothed the body in the finest garments. They placed in the coffin the chief's blankets, his gun, his supply of powder and lead, his bow and arrows, his kettle, his platter, his tomahawk, his pipe, his mirror, some collars of beads, and all the presents which were made at his death according to custom. They imagined that with this outfit he would make his journey more happily to the other world, and would be better received by the great chiefs of the nation, who would conduct him into a place of delights. While the coffin was being prepared, the relatives of the dead person assisted at the ceremony by chanting in lugubrious tones, and beating time with a stick to which they had attached many rattles.

In his letters to his relatives Father Rasle told them of his engrossing task of the study of the Abenaki language. He wrote that it was very difficult to learn, as the Indians spoke gutturally from the throat, and made no movement of the lips. He had spent a considerable time in their cabins in order to become familiar with their speech. It was necessary to pay great attention in order to conjecture what they were saying. Sometimes, he wrote, when he repeated the words it made the Indians laugh. After about five months of intensive study, he could readily understand all the terms, but could not express himself very well. He chose some of the more intelligent of his Indians, and asked them to interpret some of the articles of the catechism into their language. He wrote this down, and gradually compiled a dictionary of the language, and a catechism which contained the principles and mysteries of religion. As an example of the beauty of expression of the Indian language, Rasle said that if he asked, 'Why has God created you?' the Indian would reply, 'The Great Spirit has thought, "Let them know me, let them love me, let them honour me, and let them obey me, for then I shall make them enter into my glorious felicity." '

Father Rasle had been at Norridgewock for many years, and the English felt that his great influence over the Indians was paramount in instigating the attacks on the English settlements. They believed that it was he who had initiated a move made by the Indians in 1721, when a large number of them, in a fleet of canoes, appeared at the mouth of the Kennebec River and informed the English there that they must vacate the territory which they were occupying, or they would be destroyed. Father Rasle is said to have accompanied this delegation, and from this time resentment and anger against him grew ever more bitter. It was resolved that the priest must be removed at all costs. The French were claiming the Kennebec River as their Western boundary, while the English insisted it was the St. John River, the present boundary between Maine and Canada. They accused Rasle and his Indians of trespassing on English territory, but also, more serious than this, that he was inciting the Indians to wipe out their settlements. The Boston Puritans were well aware of the priest's influence and teachings, and in June 1700 the General Court of Massachusetts had resolved that 'all Jesuit priests and Popish missionaries' must be banished from the Province and perpetually imprisoned. When a high price was set on Rasle's head, his Indians guarded him carefully and constantly so that he could never be captured.

Father Rasle was aware that his life was in constant danger. He was advised to leave Norridgewock for the safety of Quebec, but refused. He would not desert his faithful Indians and said, 'Nothing but death shall separate me from my flock.' In 1723 matters came to a head. After a series of bloodthirsty raids by the Indians, an expedition was sent to Norridgewock to seize Father Rasle. The attempt failed and the priest managed to escape, and the only trophy Colonel Westbrook, the leader of the expedition, could bring back was Rasle's strong-box. This contained the dictionary he had com-

piled, and among other correspondence, letters from the
Governor of Canada, Monsieur Vaudreuil. In one letter
Vaudreuil urged Rasle 'to push on the Indians with all
imaginable zeal against the English.' The duplicity of
the Governor astounded the English when they read the
correspondence contained in Rasle's box. A letter was
sent by the English Governor, Samuel Shute, to Vaudreuil
letting him know he was now aware of the part he was
playing in inciting the Indians, and requesting a termination of this. In the summer of 1724, Captains Harmon and
Moulton, together with a large force of men and three
Mohawk guides, sailed up the river, and leaving their
boats, stealthily approached the village. The advance was
so swift and silent that the Indians were surprised and
surrounded. Captain Jeremiah Moulton, a native of York,
was a skilful Indian fighter. He had good reason to hate
the Indians, for his mother and father had been massacred in the Indian attack on York when he was a child.
However, Moulton gave strict instructions that Father
Rasle was not to be harmed, but to be captured alive and
taken to Boston. However, in the fighting which followed,
the priest was killed, and the braves who had tried
desperately to protect him shared his fate.

The French were angry at the news of the revered
priest's death, and Monsieur Vaudreuil sent a letter to
Governor Dummer of Massachusetts. In reply, Dummer
wrote, 'As to what you say relating to the death of Father
Rasle, the Jesuit, which you set forth as barbarous and
inhuman, I readily acknowledge that he was slain among
others of our enemies at Norridgewock, when instead of
preaching peace, love and friendship, agreeable to the
doctrines of the Christian religion, he has been a constant
and notorious fomentor and incendiary to the Indians, to
kill, burn and destroy, as flagrantly appears in many
original letters and manuscripts I have of his by me, and
when in open violation of an Act of Parliament in Great
Britain and the laws of this Province strictly forbidding

Jesuits to reside or teach within the British Dominions, he has not only resided, but also once and again appeared at the head of a great number of Indians in a hostile manner, threatening and insulting, as also publicly assaulting the subjects of His British Majesty. I say, if after all, such an incendiary has happened to be slain in the heat of action among our open and declared enemies, surely none can be blamed thereof but himself, nor can any safeguard from you or any other justify him in such proceedings.'

James Phinney Baxter, in his book *The Pioneers of New France in New England* (1894), made the strongest indictment against Father Rasle that any one has ever drawn, but wrote of him, 'We can but admire the calm radiance of Rasle upon the protection of a higher power, and his entire devotion to what he considered his duty. He was a man of heroic courage, of an earnest and self-sacrificing spirit, possessed indeed of qualities, which, in spite of some of his misconceptions of the real spirit of Christianity, entitle him to a measure of respect and admiration.'

Delegations from the Penobscot, Passamaquoddy, and Canadian tribes of Indians were present when in August, 1833, Bishop Fenwick of Boston delivered an address when a permanent monument was placed over this undoubtedly remarkable priest's grave. The inscription reads:

> Father Sebastian Rasle, a native of France, a missionary of the Society of Jesus, at first preaching to the Illinois and Hurons; afterwards for 34 years to the Abenakis, in faith and charity; a true disciple of Christ, undaunted by the danger of arms, often testifying that he was ready to die for his people; at length this best of pastors fell amidst arms at the destruction of the village at Norridgewock and the ruins of his own church on this spot, on the 23rd of August, 1724, A.D.

The ravages of decades of warring had left the Indians in a sad plight. They had lost their best young warriors. They had been unable to plant and harvest their usual crops in preparation for the long Winters because of the raids made upon their villages by the settlers. They were sick, discouraged, and starving. Any terms of peace seemed better to them than continuing further warfare. In 1725 Governor Dummer of Massachusetts came to Maine to meet the native chiefs, and arrange the conclusion of a peaceful settlement. The document was drawn up to be signed by the Indians as a practically complete surrender, and was known as 'Dummer's Treaty.' As soon as the treaty was signed a revival of interest in immigration into the Province began. There was immediately an increase in the population of the towns. New settlements sprang up, and trade increased greatly. In 1759 the principal fortress of the French at Quebec fell and the power of France in the New World was over. With the withdrawal of French control and influence, the possibility of any sustained warfare on the part of the Indians against the colonists became almost negligible, and at last the settlers could live and sleep in peace and safety.

During the next twelve years, until the beginning of the Revolution, there was a great upsurge of political excitement in the colonies. The cost of sending large armies and fleets of ships to America during the French and Indian wars had put England into debt. The people of England were bearing the brunt of this with a large increase in taxes, and there was a strong feeling that now the colonies were growing in wealth and population they should help to pay for the cost of their own defence. However, in Maine, as elsewhere, a feeling of dissatisfaction had been growing. The people objected strongly to this imposition of taxes, and to restrictions which prevented them from trading freely.

The Stamp Act was the first tax law to infuriate the Maine colonists. These stamps had to be placed on all legal documents such as wills and deeds. Some of the citizens of Falmouth (now Portland) went to the collectors' offices and destroyed the stamps. A few years after this the port of Boston was closed because the citizens refused to pay a tax on tea. A group of rebels had boarded the ships there and had thrown the tea into the harbour. Trade came to a standstill and people began to need food. Maine responded to the drastic situation by sending three hundred cords of wood, food, money, and other supplies to Boston. When a messenger rode into Maine with news of the battle there which was to start the Revolution, a company of men from York set out the next morning on the long march to Boston, to help in the fight for freedom and independence.

Several incidents involving the British occurred in Maine, and the small towns there suffered more in the Revolution than any other part of New England. In 1775 a fleet of English ships arrived at Falmouth (Portland) and demanded that the people give up all their arms. When they refused to do this, the Commander, Captain Henry Mowatt, ordered that the town should be evacuated. The town was then bombarded and more than four hundred buildings were destroyed, and about two thousand people were made homeless. An attack on the town of Machias was defeated and a British ship captured. One of the most famous episodes of the whole Revolution was that of the expedition led by Benedict Arnold against Quebec in 1775. After a long, cruel march, during which Arnold lost half of his eleven hundred men, he crossed overland into Canada and was defeated overwhelmingly at Quebec. Arnold's march was largely through Maine, and in recent years, many boulders with suitably inscribed bronze plates have been placed to mark his route, through what was then an almost unbroken wilderness. A thousand Maine men were at Valley Forge during the fateful Winter of 1777-1778. The long hard years of the French and Indian wars had provided invaluable military experience, and many Maine residents rose to positions of leadership during the Revolution.

The greatest danger to Maine came in 1779 when the British seized Castine. A naval force was sent to drive them out, but without success. When the Peace Treaty was finally signed in 1783, the British ships and troops moved out of Castine, and the long struggle was over.

After the Revolution ended, the population of Maine increased rapidly, and spread over the entire Province. Good farmland and timberland could be bought from Massachusetts for a very low price. An abundance of good timber and good harbours encouraged shipbuilding, and trade began to expand. The people of Maine were able to trade for other commodities they needed with their lumber and fish. Gradually the roads improved, and two-wheel and four-wheel carts came into use. Previously, travel by horseback was the most widely used method of getting around. Travel by stagecoach developed soon after the Revolution, and in 1803 the first stage, drawn by four horses and carrying mail and passengers, was started. One of the passengers about this time wrote, 'The mail coach is a large, clumsy vehicle carrying twelve passengers. It is cluttered with large mail bags which are greatly swollen by the bulk of newspapers. A large roll of leather was let down on each side in bad weather as a substitute for glass windows.' Previously, horsemen with saddlebags had carried most of the mail. Envelopes were not used. Instead, the writing paper was folded and sealed with sealing wax, and the name and address were written on the outside. The person who received the letter paid for it — not the person who wrote it, for it might never be delivered.

The stagecoach driver was a really important person. He wore smart clothes, a fancy tailored waistcoat, a tall hat and gloves. He was usually a great raconteur, and as he was a much travelled man he had plenty to talk about. As he went from one place to the next he collected all the latest news. He announced his arrival with a long, loud blast on his posthorn, then with the horses setting off at a full gallop, he started on his journey. When the rail-roads were built later, stagecoach travel declined rapidly.

The old tin pedlar, too, was an integral part of the Maine scene of those days. A newspaper account gave an interesting and colourful picture of this familiar part of Maine life:

> At first he peddled his wares in a basket, but when a particular type of wagon was perfected, the tin-pedlar with his well-known qualities of wit and imagination, and trading ability, really came into his own. He rode in a box-like vehicle of flaming red, and like the White Knights of old he was surrounded by gleaming metal ware. At the rear of his van there stood erect like sentinels, a row of new brooms, and below was a rack bulging with gunny sacks. The mysterious interior of his vehicle was reached by little doors through which he would thrust a groping arm in search of hidden treasures not exposed to view. He rode on a lofty seat, and from long usage it sagged precipitously to one side, as he bulged comfortably over the edge. He never wore a coat, and his waistcoat was ornamented by a heavy watch chain. From one upper pocket appeared a strange assortment of articles, among others a pencil or two, a comb, a toothbrush, and a row of cigars. He did not hawk his wares with a rasping voice, and he rode his creaking van with regal dignity, and offered business with regal favour, and then only to the elect. His arrival at a lonely farm-house was a thrilling moment. All work was suspended and the entire family gathered about him. He knew everyone within a cir-cuit of miles, and he brought the latest information of births, marriages and deaths, fires, and lesser items of more intimate interest. When the time was ripe he leisurely descended from his cart and then came an exciting time of barter. The desired articles were unhooked from the van and laid upon the grass, and then came a battle of wits, as old rags, papers, bottles, scrap iron, etc. was exchanged for the tin wares, and the deal was completed with satisfaction on both sides.

To an adult the visit of the pedlar meant gossip, news from distant places, and perhaps messages sent from friends along his route. To the children, the pedlar personified romance. He brought with him a magical connection with the world beyond their horizon. He told them thrilling adventure tales, and sometimes gave them gifts of candy and little souvenirs. Often the pedlar could play the jew's harp or the fiddle, and an enjoyable evening was spent with the whole family sitting around the fireside singing. Some pedlars pushed their goods in two-wheeled carts, others rode a single horse with a trunk swinging from each side of the saddle. After 1800 when roads were somewhat improved, carts of varying sizes, drawn by one or more horses became popular. The carts were always brightly painted. Some were bright green, others were red, and some were elegant in black and gold. These carts were miniature stores on wheels, and decorated as they were like gaudy circus wagons, could be seen approaching from a long way off.

A pedlar's life was not an easy one. He had to be his own doctor, his own cook, and his own mechanic. Sometimes it was difficult for him to find somewhere to sleep, and many camped out of doors, sleeping beside a brook or inside a haystack. Nathaniel Hawthorne wrote of his meeting with a pedlar when he travelled from Northampton to Worcester, Massachusetts by stagecoach. He wrote, 'The pedlar was good-natured and communicative, and spoke very frankly about his trade, which he seemed to like better than farming. He spoke of trials of temper to which pedlars are subjected, but said that it was necessary to be forbearing, because the same road must be travelled again and again.'

Money was scarce in those days, especially in rural areas, but every farm wife could find something she no longer wanted, which the pedlar would take in exchange for a piece of tinware. The list of goods acceptable for barter included feathers, lard, preserved fruit, maple syrup, beeswax, glass, old silver and gold, and woven cloth. A typical pedlar's call would be, 'I'll take old copper, old brass, old iron and pewter, old rags, anything except cash and old maids.' What a pity that we today can never see the scarlet of the pedlar's van on our horizon, and that he, too, is only a colourful memory of bygone days.

The church continued to be the centre of each community, and the meeting place of friends. Between the two Sunday sermons there was an interval during which the men would gather and compare notes on farm work and politics, and the women and young girls would congregate in order to gossip, to share recipes, and to proudly show off a new dress.

In old records of the town of Saco, Maine, there is a fascinating description of some of the churchgoers of those days:

> Archibald Smith, the bell-ringer, was red-faced, with a back as straight as the inside of a barrel stave. 'Squire' Vaughan, full of courtly grace, walked to his seat with great dignity of bearing. Mark Came hurried in with a bustling, business air. Tobias Lord, with a shock of bushy white hair surmounting his towering forehead, reached his pew with resolute, formidable stride. 'Major' Hobson moved down the aisle with a moderate, swinging gait. Abram L. Came was very erect, serious and dignified. 'Jim' Field wore side whiskers curled about his cheek. Ivor Clark's suit of 'pepper-and-salt' always appeared strained. Simon Palmer wore his front hair 'banged', while Deacon Leavitt exposed a shining crown. 'Uncle Daniel' McCorrison moved at a snail pace, and snored during sermon time. Horatio Bryant invariably took a morning nap in church. Little Jonah Johnston was bedangled in a long, blue, swallow-tailed coat, and was never without a tear in his eye. Joseph Decker, portly and serious looking, was as regular as a clock in his habits, but boiling over with pawky humour. Mrs. Wells, with her gold-bowed spectacles, and Mrs. Butler, the teacher, were full of grace and politeness.

In 1792, a Mr Jonathan Hyde wrote about the progress taking place, and described the town of Bath. He wrote:

> There were but few houses scattered along the river in little green openings. Many little sloops and single-deck schooners loaded with lumber were upon the water. Bath, or Long Reach, was chiefly pasture, covered with trees and bushes. A few stores, and a very few houses existed. The meeting house was one and a half miles back from the river at Witch Spring. A few farms were cleared, and vessels were building, with little villages starting up. The inhabitants at and near Bath were generally industrious, rather rough in manners, fond of a row — many would work hard

by day and be drunk by night. A few were reputable, and some were pious. The females were civil to strangers, not generally very handsome, and not overstocked with neatness. Churches were few, and schools were scarce to find. People were catching fish and rolling rocks off their fields; shipbuilding and agriculture occupied the inhabitants. Brawn was the order of the day.

With the rapid growth in trade and population, Maine citizens began to talk about separation from Massachusetts and becoming a State. Massachusetts did not want to lose Maine, and tried to keep the people in her Northern province contented by building new roads and dropping taxes on the wild lands where people were settling. Many Maine citizens felt that the seat of government was too far away. Important legal matters or disputes over land titles often required a journey to Boston, and the journey was a long one, and the travelling difficult. In 1816 the Massachusetts General Court decided that if a sufficient number of Maine citizens voted for separate statehood in the next election it would be granted. However, there were some people who were not sure that Maine was ready for such a step, and others who did not care one way or the other, so that there were not enough votes in favour of separation. The people who wanted statehood kept working for it, and on March 15th, 1820, Maine became the twenty third state in the Union.

Maine's noted historian, William D. Williamson, closed his *History of the State of Maine* (1832) with the words:

An age is now unfolded to the enjoyment of free religion and to education and the arts; — interests which form the chief glory of a community and of man. Is the visitor surprised to find with what rapidity the forest has been converted into cultivated farms and populous towns? Then may the spirit of future enterprise show that we consider the work of improvement and true greatness only commenced.

Chapter 7

Timber - r - r - r!

After church one lovely morning in mid-Summer one of our church members, an ex-colonel in the United States Air Force, who now  among his other activities operates a flight school in Bangor, asked me, 'How would you like to come for a trip this afternoon?' I had never been in a small plane before and the conditions for flying were perfect, so I accepted the invitation. After lunch we drove to the air-port and walked on to the tarmac where the plane stood waiting. It was a four-seater, and looked very small in comparison to the large jets I flew in each year on my visit back to England to see my family. I climbed into the front seat next to the pilot, while his wife and daughter sat behind. The plane taxied along the runway and soon lifted smoothly and easily into the air. As we rose higher and higher I glanced down, and as I did so, suddenly realised just how close I was to the door. I hoped the door wouldn't suddenly fly open — that the lock had been securely fastened. I also began to wish I hadn't eaten such a big lunch. Just as I was beginning to relax, my friend the pilot said, 'Here, you take the controls.' I laughed nervously and said, 'You're joking.' Without a word he took his hand from the controls and told me what I had to do to keep the stick and rudder steady. I did exactly as he said. What else could I do? At first the plane bucked wildly up and down. My friends sitting behind laughed uproariously whenever the plane dipped suddenly or shot upward. Gradually, as I became calmer and more confident, so did the plane. In the end I actually began to enjoy it. However, I was relieved when the experienced pilot took over and I was able to enjoy the terrain over which we were flying. As I gazed below I began to realise just how vast the forested area of Maine really is, and how sparsely populated. In a State the size of England there are just about one million people. There are ten million people in London alone. We flew over mile after mile of the dark green forest-land interspersed here and there with the splashes of blue which were some of Maine's two thousand odd lakes and rivers. No wonder lumbering was and always has been Maine's principal industry. No wonder it is known as the Pine Tree State, and no wonder, too, that its magnificent coastline, its tree-fringed lakes and lovely Acadia National Park annually entice hordes of 'out of Staters' to come and 'get away from it all' in Maine — Vacationland.

Soon we returned, and were flying low over Orono. I could see the church, the school, the Parsonage. There was a brown car standing outside the house — ours was cream-coloured. I wondered who was visiting. We landed and I thanked my friends for a thrilling flight. I shall never forget it. I had learned a lot, too. From the air it was easier to appreciate the fact that three quarters of Maine is still densely forested despite three centuries of foresting.

At the back of our red wooden Parsonage there is a sloping, wooded area, at the end of which there is a steep incline. At the foot of this there is a railway track, and at regular intervals throughout the day a strident hooter and a clanging bell signal the coming of the freight trains. Laden with thousands of cords of timber they snake steadily on their way to the huge paper mills. There is something warm and friendly in their regularity and continuity, and I found myself waiting expectantly for their coming.

Early English navigators were greatly impressed at the sight of the towering white pines which they could see along the coast and rivers of Maine. They realised that in these vast, magnificent forests there was an inexhaustible supply of masts, spars, and ship-building material of all kinds which England needed for her Navy. They returned with glowing accounts of this 'wooden treasure' and it was not long after the first settlements that the tall pines were being sent across the ocean to the shipyards of England.

Samuel Pepys, who was Clerk of the Acts at the Admiralty, recorded in his diary on December 3rd, 1666, 'There is also the very good news come of New England ships come home safe to Falmouth with masts for the King, which is a blessing mighty unexpected, and without which (if for nothing else) we must have failed next year. But, God be praised for thus much fortune, and send us the continuance of His favours in other things.' Pepys was able, later, to show the King at the dockyard a New England tree measuring thirty nine inches in diameter which was being made into a mast for the Royal Sovereign. There have been accounts of trees which measured as much as two hundred and sixty four feet in length and six feet in diameter.

Maine became known as 'the Mast Country', and her timber resources were highly regarded by the Admiralty. Restrictions were imposed on the cutting of the larger pines, and by the Colonial Charter of 1691 all trees with a diameter of twenty four inches or more were reserved to the Crown for the use of the Royal Navy. Severe penalties were imposed on those who took any mast tree without a license. Some of the pioneer lumbermen resented these restrictions and hacked down any tree they chose. In order to enforce the law a Royal Surveyor was appointed with four deputies. Their duties entailed long and arduous journeys into often uncharted and unexplored wilderness. They travelled along the coast and up the rivers, marking the King's trees with a broad arrow, the symbol used to identify Government property. This angered the settlers even more, and some historians have asserted that as far as Maine was concerned, the seeds of the Revolution began in the forests, and in the contests between the lumbermen and the King's Surveyor.

Up until the 1800's large tracts of land were covered principally with pine trees. However, the woodsman's axe as well as many devastating fires which swept the forests from time to time, sadly depleted the pines. As well as having millions of acres of the finest timber lands Maine has the advantage of having numerous rivers with easy access to them. The Penobscot River penetrates into the heart of vast acres of forest land, and therefore it seemed only natural that the lumber industry should be centred there. During the period from 1830-1860 there were said to have been ten thousand men engaged in lumbering on the Penobscot alone. Saw mills grew and multiplied and the city of Bangor, at the head of the Penobscot navigation, became a city of great importance in the lumber industry. *The New Orleans Bulletin* of 1834 described the Bangor of those days:

> The city of Bangor in the State of Maine is among the Eastern wonders of the world. But a few years ago — a very few years — it was but a humble, unimportant village. In 1830 it had not a population of three thousand we believe. Now it is supposed to have eight thousand inhabitants, and is the second town in the State in population. But a short time ago the country all around was a wilderness. Now busy and thriving villages are opening up in all directions and the wilderness is blooming like the rose.

In the early days Bangor was known as the Conduskeag Plantation and about forty five families had settled there. In 1786 the Reverend Seth Noble, who had been a clergyman in New Brunswick, came to Conduskeag with his wife and three children. Noble, a native of Westfield, Massachusetts, had been a Methodist before becoming a Congregationalist. He was a patriot and had become a chaplain serving under Colonel John Allen during the Revolution. When the war ended the Government gave Noble a tract of land in what is now Eddington, and he settled there with his family in 1786. There was no organized church then on either side of the river Penobscot, but a group of religious people were eager to employ a minister, and it was felt that the Reverend Seth Noble was just the man for the job. An arrangement was made with him and it was agreed that he would receive a stipend of four hundred dollars a year. At this time Noble was forty three years of age, a thin faced, spare man of medium height, with a fresh complexion. Apparently he was a lively man, quick and nervous in his movements, and is said to have been a very good preacher, eloquent and gifted in prayer. He has been described as 'a man of energy', possessed a fine tenor voice, enjoyed singing himself and taught singing, too. One of his deacons, William Boyd, once said of him, 'One would think when he was in the pulpit he ought never to leave it.' Another record of the statement modifies this by prefacing it with, 'One would think when he was out of the pulpit he should never enter it.'

This, then, was the man whose induction service was held on September 10th, 1786, on a platform laid on barrels, in a grove of oak trees overlooking the Penobscot River, in the presence of a large crowd of people. After a year of Noble's ministry, however, the initial enthusiasm in the community began to wane as the people began to lose respect for him. They felt that sometimes his conversation was too frivolous and that he lacked some of the qualities necessary for the dignity of his calling. He drank heavily, too, and would tell improper stories, laughing uproariously. At first efforts and plans were made to build a meeting house but with the people's waning interest this did not materialize. It was said, too, that after the death of Noble's first wife in 1791 he courted a widow Emery, and moved into her house before the marriage, thus inviting criticism of his moral conduct. Eventually the people grew tired of his drinking habits and his 'moral obliquity in another respect', and his ministerial labours in Bangor came to an end.

However, it was Noble was was responsible for Bangor receiving its name. In 1790 he sailed from Bangor to Boston to present to the General Court a petition for the

settlement's incorporation as a town. A previous petition
had not been granted. It had been intended originally
that Sunbury should be the plantation's new name, but
Seth Noble was so fond of the hymn tune known by the
name Bangor that he thought this would be a more fitting
name for the town and substituted it. The Act incorporating the town of Bangor was passed on February
25th, 1791.

Bangor seems to have been unfortunate in its choice of
ministers in these early days. A town meeting on the 4th
of April, 1796 appointed a committee to hire a minister.
However, it seems that a selection was not made until the
year 1800 when the Reverend James Boyd was appointed.
The town of Bangor and the Congregationalists of Orrington and Hampden united and issued a call to Boyd. The
ordination took place in Orrington, after which there was
a feast at a Madam Holyoke's, when it is said 'new rum
and other liquors flowed freely.' It is said, too, that 'the
Reverend Mr. Boyd gave infallible evidence of their
intoxicating qualities.' A poet of the time took advantage
of Boyd's over-indulgence and wrote scathingly of him:

A minister, a drunken cur as ever yet was seen,
Came from the west and built his nest down by Conduskeag
[Stream.

Unfortunately, it became obvious very soon that Boyd
was a bad choice, for at the end of one year the town
called a council of ministers from other areas to try him on
six charges — some of them allegations of gross im-
morality. Mr. Amos Patten who was Town Clerk at the
time made a record of the proceedings, but he was so
reticent about revealing details of the 'six heavy charges'
that he made instead the note 'decency might blush
at recording them.' After investigating fully the causes
of complaint the council unanimously agreed that Mr.
Boyd's usefulness as a minister of the Gospel was at an
end. Thus was a second minister of Bangor dismissed,

and with him, apparently, all desire to appoint another, at least for a time.

By the Fall of 1811 the Congregationalists of the area began to desire eagerly once again that a permanent church should be formed there. Although few in number they set about the task courageously and went forward with a strong faith. Judge William D. Williamson was one of the prime movers of the venture, as was William Boyd who later became the first deacon of the new church. He it was, of course, who had been a deacon at the time of the Reverend Seth Noble. The new church was fully constituted on November 27th, 1811. The Reverend Harvey Loomis, a young man of about twenty six years of age, had been called to be pastor of the new church, and became the only settled minister in Bangor for the next fourteen years. He has been described as 'eminently a lovable man.' He was apparently amiable and genial, a man whose life was true and consistent. His appeals to the irreligious were 'so honest and earnest that large numbers were added to the church, and religion was respected and the morals of the community greatly improved.' In an historical sketch of the church published in 1856 his sermons were described as 'short, pithy, pointed, direct, aimed at the conscience, and delivered in an interesting and impressive manner.'

On Sunday, January 2nd, 1825, the Reverend Harvey Loomis walked from his home to the church in a heavy snow-storm. The ascent to the church was quite steep, and the deep snow made progress difficult. Loomis was exhausted by the time he reached the church. He entered the pulpit, but before he had even started the sermon, collapsed and died. The shock of his sudden death was emphasised when it was discovered that the text he had chosen to preach on, on this first Sunday of the year were the words of Jeremiah, Chapter 28, verse 16, — 'This year thou shalt die.' Thus Bangor suffered an irreparable loss and greatly mourned the man they had so greatly esteemed. *The History of Penobscot County, Maine* (1882) said of Loomis, 'He died at his post with his armor on.' He had certainly laid a firm foundation for the future of the church in Bangor.

Henry David Thoreau described the Bangor of 1846 graphically in *The Maine Woods*. He wrote:

> There stands the city of Bangor, fifty miles up the Penobscot, at the head of navigation for vessels of the largest class, the principal lumber depot on this continent, with a population of twelve thousand, like a star on the edge of night, still hewing at the forests of which it is built, already overflowing with the luxuries and refinement of Europe, and sending its vessels to Spain, to England and to the West Indies for its groceries, — and yet only a few axe-men have gone 'up river' into the howling wilderness which feeds it. . . . Twelve miles in the rear are Orono and the Indian Island, the home of the Penobscot tribe . . . and sixty miles above, the country is virtually unmapped and unexplored, and still there waves the virgin forest of the New World.

Elsewhere in his journal Thoreau wrote,

> Within a dozen miles of Bangor we passed through the villages of Stillwater and Oldtown, built at the falls of the Penobscot, which furnish the principal power by which the Maine woods are converted into lumber. The mills are built directly over and across the river. There were, in 1837, as I read, two hundred and fifty saw mills on the Penobscot and its tributaries above Bangor, the greater part of them in this immediate neighbourhood, and they sawed two hundred millions of feet of boards annually.

The ships which came to Bangor for lumber were so numerous that it has been said that on many occasions it was possible to walk across the harbour from Bangor to Brewer on their decks. In 1860 there were 3,376 vessels arriving and departing from the port, and in July of that year sixty vessels arrived in Bangor in one day within a period of two hours. The *Bangor Daily Whig and Courier* of June 16th, 1837 contained the announcement, 'More than one hundred vessels are now lying in this port, all of them having arrived within four days.' Below and above Bangor the river was never empty. From the mills at Orono and Old Town came long rafts of sawn lumber floating down river to the docks, to be taken apart board by board and stowed into the holds of the ships. For many years, therefore, Bangor was known as one of the biggest lumber markets in the world. As the pine supply became gradually depleted due to the woodsman's axe and the many destructive fires which swept over the forests from time to time, the importance of Bangor declined. The white pine has disappeared as a commercial lumber tree in New England, but it will live forever in men's imagination and memory.

The quiet, orderly Bangor of today bears little resemblance to the boisterous, rip-roaring city of those days. It is almost impossible to imagine now the hordes of merchants and sailors from all parts of the world who swarmed about the city then. Together with the enormous, tough, rumbustious lumbermen and river drivers who thronged into Bangor after a heavy Winter's work, pockets bulging with accumulated wages and ready for anything, it sometimes created an explosive situation. For about fifty years in the mid-nineteenth century a section of the city which became known as 'the devil's half-acre' flourished. In this area were the taverns, grog shops, lodging houses and brothels. Here it was that the tall timber men drank vast quantities of rum, swapped yarns, indulged in fist fights and sought out their women. Many taverns had open-topped barrels with chained dippers. The price of the rum was a nickel a dipper.

After months of hard and dangerous work in Spartan conditions these men of the woods were certainly ready for relaxation, and they set out to enjoy themselves wholeheartedly. The tavern floors were pock-marked with deep scars from the caulked boots they wore, and the streets echoed with their roistering songs. It is said that the 'ladies of the town' were always ready for the men's arrival, and one of them, a notorious Fan Jones, built and operated her famous Sky Blue House. She was a shrewd woman. On the outside of her house was a huge chimney. This was painted a vivid blue which was never allowed to fade, and was repainted twice a year. The chimney was so placed that it became a landmark for the women-hungry loggers coming down river from the woods. Fan did extremely well by this service in ensuring that no man could possibly lose his way in Bangor with her house to guide him.

The lumbermen played a great part in America's history, although less has been written about them than of the cowboy and other pioneering types. They were hardy and fearless, a colourful breed of men with their beards, their red-checked woollen shirts, grey pants, woollen caps and heavy boots. In his book, *Adventures in the Wilds of America* (1856), Charles Lanman described the lumbermen of that time:

> They are a young and powerfully built race of men, mostly New Englanders, generally unmarried, and, though rude in their manner, and intemperate, are quite intelligent. They seem to have a passion for their wild and toilsome life, and judging from their dress, I should think possess a fine eye for the comic and fantastic. The entire apparel of an individual usually consists of a pair of gray pantaloons and two red flannel shirts, a pair of long boots, and a woollen covering for the head, and all these things are worn at one and the same time. . . . Their wages vary from twenty to thirty dollars per month, and they are chiefly employed by the lumber merchants of Bangor, who furnish them with the necessary supplies.

Before the logging operations began, the potentiality of the terrain was explored by the lumber merchant himself, or through an agent. This operation became known as 'cruising' and was usually carried out in the Fall. The timber cruiser and a companion, sometimes two, set out with the necessary provisions, usually consisting of ship's bread, salt pork, tea, sugar or molasses, cooking utensils, blankets, an axe, a gun and some ammunition. These were usually loaded on to a bateau and off they set. Sometimes they penetrated about two hundred miles into the wilderness interior, in areas never before trodden by the feet of white men. Selecting a suitable spot near a gushing spring or gurgling stream they pitched their tent. This usually consisted of a frame of slender poles, lightly covered on top and at each side with long boughs. The front was left open and a watch fire would glow comfortingly in the deep darkness of the forest night. After a meal of roasted salt pork, bread, and hot, sweet tea, the men would smoke their pipes, then throw their weary limbs onto beds of soft tree boughs. The danger of a prowling bear or wolf was always there, and the night sounds of the forest's other numerous wild inhabitants were all around them as they slept. An animal belonging to the cat family lived in the deep forests then. It was known as 'the Indian devil' (in the Indian language 'lunk soos'). This ferocious animal was a terror to the Indians — an animal to be greatly feared and dreaded. The next morning the men arose refreshed and ready for the day's tasks. The density of the forest and the uneven surface of the area made reconnaissance difficult. To overcome this obstacle one of the men climbed to the top of a lofty tree. From such a tree-top suitable areas for lumbering could be discovered. The man at the top pointed out the direction of a suitable site, while the man at the base of the tree marked the direction by means of a compass, a necessary part of any woodsman's equipment.

After spending several days in search of suitable trees, estimating the quality of the timber, determining where the streams and sections of the river suitable for driving the lumber were, they mapped out the areas where the logging roads were to be cut. They planned, too, the best location for the camp site. The cruisers then retraced their steps to the place where they had left their bateau and returned once again to civilization.

Now that the territory had been explored and the land

from which the logs were to be cut and hauled determined, permits had to be obtained from the State or land owner in order to secure exclusive rights to cut timber within the bounds of the grant for a stipulated price.

Among other preparations for the Winter operations was the 'putting up' of large quantities of meadow hay. This was essential for the subsistence of the teams of oxen employed in procuring the lumber. Large crews of men set out with farming implements to the immediate vicinity of the forest, where there were large tracts of meadow grass. There the men set to work making and stacking the hay to be used during the long Winter months. These stacks were later removed by boat before the waters froze, or later by sleds drawn on the ice. The men's lives were made intolerable over this hay-making period by millions of bloodthirsty flies which swarmed incessantly over the fields. These atrocious little menaces would infiltrate the men's clothing and cause severe irritation. One rather drastic palliative for this affliction was to shave the head high above the ears and spread on layers of tar mixed with bear grease or lard.

Once the preliminaries were settled, arrangements were made at once to build the Winter camp in the already selected location. A central position in regard to the timber and water facilities, and the locating of roads had all had to be taken into consideration. Once this was done the top strata of leaves and turf had to be removed from the area where the cabin was to be erected, in order to avoid the risk of fire. Whilst this was being done other men felled trees and cut them into suitable lengths. Larger logs were formed into a square, with the ends notched together, then one tier after another was laid until the requisite height was reached. The roof was made from shingles three to four feet in length, cut from spruce and cedar trees. These were secured in place by laying a heavy pole across each tier. The roof was finally covered with boughs of fir, spruce and hemlock, so that

in the coldest weather the camp was warm and dry.
The crevices between the logs in the walls were tightly
packed with moss and earth, so that no draught could
possibly penetrate.

This done, a shed was then built for the oxen. This
was known as the hovel. It had a flooring made from
small poles laid closely together and smoothed with
an adz. The crevices in the walls were plastered with clay
or ox manure, which ensured that the animals were
kept warm and dry. A temporary shed in front of this
served as a storage place for hay and provender.

After the completion of the men's and animals' quarters came the construction of suitable roads. These
usually began at the landing place on the river bank and
were cut back toward the principal part of the timber to be
cut and hauled. First the undergrowth was cut and thrown
to one side, then all the trees in the area to be cleared
were cut close to the ground and disposed of. The ground
was then levelled and completely flattened, and small
poles or skids were laid across to form a good firm road
on which to haul the logs.

During the months of November and December after
the early snow, and when the ground and swamps had
frozen, a team of oxen, usually consisting of from four to
eight oxen, was made ready. They were attached to a
long sled loaded with provisions and tools, and were
accompanied by the new recruitment of hands. Leaving
the comfort of home and civilization the team moved
slowly forward to join the men who had preceded them in
order to prepare for their coming. After several days'
journeying and resting en route at suitable stopping
places, the team at last reached what was to be their new
home for the next few months. Often these camps were
almost two hundred miles into the interior of the dense
forest lands.

After a few days' respite in which to become acclimatized, work began in earnest. Each man was assigned a

particular part of the labour, and the wages were paid accordingly. The wages were regulated, too, by the ability of the individual to fulfil his task. First was the camp boss whose job it was, apart from supervising the cutting of the trees and the laying of roads, to act as banker, doctor and counsellor. Then came the choppers, who selected and felled the trees. One of these was the master-chopper. The barker and loader's job was to hew off that section of the bark from the part of the log which was to be dragged on the snow, and to assist the teamsters in loading. The swampers cut and cleared the roads through the forest to the fallen trees so that teams of oxen could move easily as they drew the logs to the river bank. The oxen were slow and sometimes cantankerous beasts but they were strong and dependable. There was, too, the teamster, or captain of the goad, and last, but certainly not least, the cook.

The men would set off at daybreak to that area of the forest where the trees were marked for cutting. Soon their axes would begin to fly, cutting deeper and deeper into the wood, until the cry 'Timber . . r . . r . . r' would echo through the forest. The men would run as the great tree groaned, then swished and cracked, finally crashing with a tremendous boom. Then for a time all would become silent again in the forest. The lumberjacks knew exactly where the chopped tree would land and could fell the trees with great precision. Sometimes, however, there were unavoidable accidents. An account in the *Bangor Daily Whig and Courier* of February 18th, 1835, described one of these:

> We understand that a man named Henry Inman of Orono was killed in the woods in the following singular manner: — he was engaged with two other lumbermen in felling a large tree, which in falling, came in contact with a decayed tree which broke, and in the rebound struck Inman a blow which fairly buried him in the snow and caused his instant death.

The hard work gave the men enormous appetites,

and vast quantities of supplies were required. Bangor became the great centre of supply in Eastern and Northern Maine. Necessary items were corn or oats for the oxen, tea, tobacco, pork, dry or salt fish, molasses, beans, flour. A typical quantity of the supplies sent annually from Bangor into the lumber camps included 50,000 barrels of flour, 250,000 bushels of corn and 6,000 barrels of pork. Camp utensils such as frying pans, dishes, pans, etc., were advertised in Bangor newspapers. In Bangor, too, woodsmen's outfits, hats, boots, blankets, moccasins, and several types of axes were offered for sale.

In the early days the lumbermen's food was simple and monotonous. Often they would have a steady menu of pork and beans, sometimes three times a day. Strong black tea with molasses for sweetening was drunk with every meal. Thoreau wrote, 'This beverage is as indispensable to the loggers as to any gossiping old woman in the land, and they no doubt derive great comfort from it.' Sometimes the menu was supplemented by fish, sometimes by venison, caribou, moose, or even bear meat (which tasted like pork). The forests abounded in wild life and the streams teemed with fish. The men had special names for the various concoctions they ate. 'Stujo' was venison, rabbit, or other meat stewed with potatoes in an iron pot. 'Dunderjunk' was a baked dish of bread, pork, and molasses. Baked beans were always a great favourite with the men. A hole was dug in the ground, a fire built in it, and the bean pot set in the hot coals. This was covered again with earth, and the supper would be cooking whilst the men worked all day. The cooks were a law unto themselves, and some of them insisted upon absolute silence during meal times.

The early logging camps were very simple and basic. There were usually no windows in these cabins, just a wooden door. In the centre of the roof there was usually a chimney of about four feet square. This was constructed of logs and plastered with clay. A fire was built directly under this on the bare earth, for warmth and cooking purposes. One section of the camp's interior was used for eating in, another for cooking, and the rest for sleeping. In the early days the men slept on the bare earth on which a thick layer of hemlock, cedar and fir boughs was strewn. Bedding usually consisted of a number of blankets sewn together, and a very large spread stuffed with cotton batting. The men would crawl beneath the coverings and huddle together for warmth. Lice, too, found a perfect resting place (and hunting ground) here.

There was certainly no shortage of firewood, and after supper each night a large fire was built to last the whole night long. It is said that the amount of wood used in building one camp fire would be enough to supply an ordinary home for a whole week. Some of the logs were so large that they burned often for twenty four hours before finally extinguishing. The fire was kept up during the night while the men slept. There was the constant hazard of flying sparks, and occasionally a tragedy occurred, when lumbermen died as a result of suffocation when fire broke out. Often, too, the smoke from the fire remained inside when the wind was in the wrong direction and did not escape through the chimney, so that the men's clothes were impregnated with the smoke and their eyes sore, too.

Usually the only article of furniture in these early camps was the 'deacon seat.' This was a sort of bench made from a log split in half, with the flat side up, with legs attached, and standing about eighteen inches from the floor. These benches were so called because in church the deacons usually sat in the front of the church, and as these seats were placed on each side of the fire, the 'deacon seat' became the bench nearest the fire in a lumber camp. Many good yarns were told by the loggers whilst sitting on these benches by the fire, and a good tall story is known as a 'deacon seater' by old Maine people. The deacon seat often served as a table, too, and the men would gather around, each dipping his bread, potato and salt pork into the spider (an outsized frying pan) to soak up the pork fat.

These rather primitive windowless cabins were improved by 1860 by the addition of a couple of windows, a floor of poles and a large cast iron box stove which stood in the centre of the room. Two-men bunks were also introduced, and the rows of bunks went the whole length of the room and often around one end. Sometimes a chair might be made from a flour barrel and there might be a rough stool, but these were the only refinements. The food improved gradually, too, and by this time there might be hot biscuits, doughnuts and gingerbread for breakfast.

Evenings in the camp were short, as the men worked from dawn to dusk, and by the time supper was over and the nightly camp-fire built up there was just a short time for relaxation before the men sank gratefully onto their couches of green boughs. After supper some men sat puffing away contentedly at their pipes or chewed tobacco. One might spend the time whittling away with a huge jack-knife at a new axe handle or a wooden toy. Others engaged in a game of cards, exchanged stories and sang ballads of home and loved ones, of death on the logging drives, and the gorgeous girls of Bangor. The men welcomed Sunday for the rest, and the opportunity it gave them to attend to necessary personal tasks. Most of all they enjoyed the extra long sleep and sometimes did not rise until mid morning or even later. After a leisurely breakfast each man was free to choose whatever interest or inclination he might enjoy. Some might wander through the forest in order to replenish their beds with fresh boughs of evergreens, others oil-stoned their axe blades in order to keep them keen. Red flannel shirts were washed and mended, pants were patched, mittens and socks were repaired, and boots were tapped and greased. There were always steaming clothes strung overhead on poles, as near the fire as possible. Letters home would be written on sheets of grubby paper. There was sometimes a deer or moose hunt, which, if successful, would provide the men with a welcome change from the usual salted provisions. The cook would sometimes make a tasty dish from a hare or partridge the men might have killed. There might be excursions into the forest, too, in search of spruce gum or timber from which to make new axe helves. The younger woodsmen would box and wrestle and indulge in various contests of skill. They would vie as to which of them was the most expert tree feller or the one who had most success with women. There were sometimes bloody fights when the men used their teeth, thumbs and boots, while the rest of the crew cheered on their favourites as they tussled together. In the evening there was usually a fiddler or accordionist in the group who would lead the singing.

Opportunities for religious services at the camp were few and far between in the early logging days, and visits from missionaries were rare. One minister, the Reverend Jotham Sewell, recorded in his memoirs in 1853 a visit to a camp on the Dead River when he ate and slept with the men and preached to them twice. His appropriate texts were 'He found him in a desert land' and 'The voice of one crying in the wilderness.' A senior at the Bangor Theological Seminary is said to have exhorted about thirty river drivers to lead a better life, and in 1872 the Reverend James Cameron of Greenville supplied bibles, testaments and tracts to about thirty logging camps in his area. The Reverend Charles Whittier, brother of the poet John Greenleaf Whittier, apparently served as a missionary to logging camps in Washington County, Maine, for many years. However, religious contact was sporadic, and in *The History of the Congregational Churches in Maine* it was noted that there was no regular religious work with the lumbermen until 1888.

On the whole, in spite of their hard life and crude living conditions, the men were healthy and hardy. The principal reason for this was believed to be the long hours of vigourous work they spent in the cold pure air. Few of the men ever suffered from colds or similar ailments. The camp's medical supplies were of a very basic, limited nature. A fresh chunk of tobacco or a slice of pork was applied directly over a cut or bruise. Beef brine was used for sprains and four tablespoonfuls of kerosene was believed to be a great tonic. Rotten pine wood was used to soothe chafed skin, and in the morning some of the men would put lard inside their socks before putting them on. A tub of lard was kept near at hand for this purpose.

All logs had to be marked before the Spring river drive, as on their way down-stream they became mingled with logs of other owners. Log marks were like cattle brands and were usually registered for their owner's protection, and in order to avoid duplication. Great ingenuity was used in inventing different symbols. There were crosses, darts, diamonds, anchors, crows' feet, letters of the alphabet, numerals, or a combination of these. The marks were chopped into the logs at both ends and were made by an axe of auger cutting into the sapwood. This required a great deal of skill.

When the long Winter showed signs of ending at last, and the deep snows began to melt, the men began to look forward with keen anticipation to getting back once again to civilization. The Winter's work of felling trees and hauling was completed and the 'breaking up' period began. This time was a joyful occasion for the men. They were exhilarated at the thought of change after the three or four months spent in the wilderness away from homes and families and the bright city lights. Everyone would be in high spirits as they loaded the long sleds with possessions and equipment. The oxen were attached to the sled and the procession moved slowly away from the camp toward home, leaving a portion of the crew behind to make the necessary preparations for the river drive. After several days' travel the team reached home and made a triumphal entry into town. Tall poles were fastened to the sled and festooned with flags made from handkerchiefs or strips torn from old red flannel shirts. Their hats were decorated with ribbons of the same material, and around their waists they might wear sashes made from red scarves. In places like Bangor the arrival of a company of these teams, sometimes amounting to forty or fifty men and an equal number of oxen caused great excitement and interest. The townspeople were aware, too, that the growth and prosperity of the town were partly due to the toil and hardship of these colourful men. A *Bangor Daily Whig and Courier* of March 1834 paints a vivid picture of the lumbermen's return to Bangor.

> The lumbermen are returning from their Winter quarters, and their departure is marked by movements somewhat similar to the breaking up of a muster or ball. The cattle are brought down in droves and carried away to be refitted by food and rest for employment another season. The weary teamsters, with long beards and tattered garments are emerging from the depths of the forest again to breathe the atmosphere of civilized life, after having been pent up through the dreary Winter months in the camps in the woods. It must be pleasure indeed for them to join their families again, and count their gains while they recount their hardships.

In the early 1800's these arrivals and those of the river-drivers were characterized by free indulgence in rum and other spirits. Liquor flowed freely and there was fighting and brawling.

In the meantime the men left behind at the camp were joined by others, and plans were made for the beginning of the river-drive. When the ice thawed in the river, ton after ton of timber was rolled into the rushing water. Some logs were too cumbersome to move easily, so the men had to leap into the swirling water in order to urge

them over the difficult places. Their feet and legs could
be numbed within a few minutes, so they would climb on
to the bank and after a short time of brisk rubbing and
stamping were ready to jump in and set to work again.

The men shouted and sang at the tops of their voices
as they jumped onto the timber, they rode with it, balancing with their poles as they made the long, turbulent
journey down-stream. It was rough and dangerous work.
The fast boiling white water swirled around, often reaching their knees. The men worked from daylight until
dusk, their feet wet all the time, as they worked in the
icy water. The logs rolled easily and were often very
slippery, so that a man needed to have the balancing
skill of a tight-rope walker. Two phrases which have
been coined from river-driving days and which remain in
common usage today are 'come hell or high water' and
'as easy as falling off a log.' There were often many
casualties on these river drives. Many men drowned,
others were crushed by heavy timbers as they jammed on
rocky ledges. A single slip might mean certain death at
any moment. A sharp bend or narrow neck in the river
could cause a jam, and a log jam could be extremely
hazardous. Sometimes one log after another would
become entangled until hundreds, even thousands,
jammed the river. A great deal of bravery and skill was
required in order to break the jam, as large masses could
rush forward suddenly and crush the driver. These
river men had great courage, skill and resolution. Their
daring and physical toughness were unequalled by any
other group of men. It seemed that the danger of the work
somehow added a kind of zest. It might take days or
even longer before the channel could be cleared. The
men would jump, cheer and yell with joy when eventually
hundreds of logs surged forward in mad confusion,
with a deafening roar which could be heard for miles.

Some of the best river men were those who had spent
their time as small boys learning to walk on floating logs

or walking the booms at the mills. The Bangor river-drivers from the Penobscot were in great demand on river drives in New England and other parts of America. They were known as the 'Bangor Tigers', drew top wages, and their fame spread as they became predominant in America's logging history.

The river-drivers' mode of life, like that of the lumber-men, was Spartan and comfortless. The men were used to working in the icy cold Spring water, were rarely ever dry, and even if a man fell in and got completely wet, he rarely changed his clothes until night time. Rum was considered a necessity on a drive, and great quantities of the liquor were consumed in order to keep out the chills which might result from the continual soaking. The men camped out on the river bank as they worked their way down river. Their bed was the bare, cold earth, with a mattress of boughs, and a blanket for covering. If it rained they used an upturned bateau for shelter. A large fire would usually be kept burning throughout the night. The boats loaded with provisions and cooking utensils moved along day by day according to the progress made by the drive. Taking these loaded boats down river, particularly along swirling waters, was a dangerous business and sometimes involved loss of provisions, or even lives. This task, therefore, was generally entrusted to the most experienced river-men. It was essential that the men should be well fed, and they usually ate four good meals a day. The usual staples in the menu were similar to those of the lumber camp, pork, beans, fish, molasses, and, of course, plenty of good strong tea. The cook set up camp at appropriate distances down-stream, and the tired, cold and hungry men were always more than ready for a welcome break from their hard and dangerous work.

When a man was killed on a drive the crew sometimes hung his boots to a tree limb to mark the spot where he had died, and occasionally erected a rough cross over the place where he was buried. The body was often placed in a coffin composed of two empty flour barrels. The body was committed to its rough burial often in silence, though if an itinerant clergyman happened to be in the vicinity the usual funeral service would be observed. For several days the men would be quiet and subdued. They no longer joked or sang as they mourned a comrade and meditated on the frailty and uncertainty of human life. However, the mood soon passed and their usual cheerfulness returned.

The men would wear caulked boots always. These spike-soled footwear came up to the knee and were constructed of strong excellent leather. As they were worn in the water the boots had to be kept well greased. The heels and soles of the boots were studded with about thirty six metal spikes about an inch long so that the wearer would be ensured of the secure footing needed on the rolling and pitching logs, and to make him safer on the booms and sluicing platforms. The owners of down-river dance halls, taverns and lodging houses were outraged at the way these boots tore up their floors, and protested vigourously. About 1900 Maine legislators enacted a law forbidding the wearing of such boots in public places. Holman Day wrote a few lines protesting the law: 'For angels can just as well shed their wings as a driver his spike-sole boots.'

There were many booms along the river to which the logs were driven. In the Penobscot River area, the largest was the main Bangor boom at Old Town. By running boom sticks from island to island and from pier to pier a vast trap was formed to catch the logs as they came downriver. There they were sorted. *The Bangor Daily Whig and Courier* of May 22nd, 1837, wrote of an incident that happened frequently, the giving way of a boom:

The main boom at the Mill Dam gave way yesterday afternoon and from six to eight thousand logs went adrift. They were passing the city all last evening. The loss will prove exceedingly heavy to individuals. The steamer Bangor was obliged to anchor in the river in consequence of the number of floating logs.

In 1858 a blacksmith, Joseph Peavey of Stillwater, watched from a bridge some river-drivers at work, trying to turn over logs with their heavy poles. At once he realised a simple improvement could be made which would facilitate their work. He went into his workshop and quickly fashioned a spike with a hinged claw on it which gripped the logs easily. A great rise in efficiency resulted from the use of the new tool, which became known as the 'peavey' after its inventor. These tools are still manufactured and used today.

The editor of the *Bangor Daily Whig and Courier* wrote of the colour of the river drive in 1835:

> The dexterity of the drivers, as they are called, is really wonderful; we saw a raft of timber with four men upon it, pass through the breach in the mill-dam works yesterday, and it was a glorious sight! — worth all the theatres, pantomimes and exhibitions of art in Christendom.

Unfortunately the days of the great logs are over. Most of the timber cut now is pulpwood from the spruce. Used in the manufacture of paper, which is now Maine's biggest industry, this is cut into lengths of four feet, and is transported by freight trains. The tall timber days belong to the past, as do the tall, colourful lumberjacks whose songs echo through the years:

> Come all ye gallant shanty boys and listen while I sing,
> We've worked six months in cruel frosts but soon we'll take our
> [fling.
> The ice is black and rotten, and the rollways are piled high,
> So boost upon your peavey sticks whilst I do tell you why:
> For it's break the rollways out, my boys, and let the big sticks
> [slide,
> And file your caulks and grease your boots and start upon the
> [drive.
> A hundred miles of water is the nearest way to town,
> So tie into the tail of her and keep her hustling down.

In Bangor today overlooking the Penobscot River, there is a thirty-one foot high statue of a bearded lumberjack wearing the typical red-checked shirt and grey trousers and woollen cap, and holding an axe and a peavey. This is the legendary figure of Paul Bunyan who typified the loggers of those bygone days. An inscription reads:

> The legendary giant woodsman is a symbol of the great era in the late 1800's during which Bangor, Maine, was acclaimed the lumber capital of the world. The statue faces the Penobscot River, which in the days of Paul Bunyan bristled with masts, as sailing vessels loaded long lumber for shipment to sea-ports around the world.

Another statue which is of bronze stands in the centre of Bangor. This depicts a group of river-drivers with their tools, breaking a log jam.

In the centre of Bangor, too, stands the famous Bangor House, which in those days flourished as one of the most colourful hotels in New England. There one could have steak or chicken for breakfast, Penobscot River salmon, venison and moose for dinner, and an open fire in one's bedroom, all included, for three dollars a day. Daniel Webster wined and dined there, as well as other colourful figures, such as Presidents Ulysses Grant and Theodore Roosevelt, the English playwright Oscar Wilde, and the prize-fighter John L. Sullivan. Now the hotel has been completely remodelled to provide accommodation for elderly citizens. There was something vital and exciting about those days which has vanished forever, a certain magic which can never return.

Of the lumbermen Fannie Hardy Eckstorm wrote:

> And I never again shall behold men looking like those I used to see when they came off the river — white and Indian crisped almost to a blackness by the sun, baked with the heat, bitten by black flies, haggard, gaunt, sore-footed, so that once their driving boots were off, their parboiled feet could endure none but the softest kid or congress cloth, and even those I have seen them remove whenever they could; and above all, sleepy, falling asleep when they talked to you, gaping from unutterable weariness, dropping into a dead slumber if left alone for a moment, and waking with a jump when anything stirred. In those days they worked day and night. . . . 'Leave us, O time, the memory of men like this.'

Chapter 8

Accident or Design?

I lived in Maine for more than eight years, and became accustomed to its moods, its patterns, its customs and its everyday life. I felt a part of Maine. It was only when I had to register as a 'resident alien' each January that I remembered that I was a 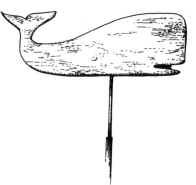 'foreigner'. On one of my annual visits to England I was asked to speak to a group of Anglican church women on any subject I cared to choose. 'I'll speak on my life as a Maine-iac,' I said casually. There was an awkward silence — an anxious look, until I reassured the poor secretary of the group that this simply meant a talk about my life in the State of Maine, and not, as it obviously must have sounded, a history of my mental state. The day of the meeting arrived, the talk was received well, and, judging by the questions which followed, the group was clearly interested. One of the women said, 'One thing puzzles me, and that is the way you speak about Maine, as if *that* were your homeland.' I was delighted that I had managed to convey the feeling of warmth and 'belonging' I have for the place I have grown to love.

It is amazing how the complex pieces of life, like a jigsaw puzzle, fit so well together. Was it accident or design that I should have been born and brought up in a town in England whence the Pilgrims sailed to a new life in New England, where I, too, was to spend some of my happiest years? Was it accident or design that the founder of the State in which I was to live, should have spent most

of his life in my home town? There were so many strange
coincidences that led me to Maine that I can't help feeling
that it was intended that I should have gone there. Ten
years before we left England, at our pastorate in the
North of England, a gipsy came to the Manse door selling
sprigs of white heather (for luck, she said). I bought one
from her, and as she turned to go, she looked piercingly
at me and said, 'One day you will live in Canada.' This
seemed highly unlikely at the time, and I soon forgot
her prophecy until the time of the 'call' to Orono, and I
realised its proximity to Canada.

Just before leaving England I read a book which made
a great impression on me. It was *Ten Fingers for God*, the
story of an English surgeon, Paul Brand, who went to
Vellore, India, after World War II in order to work
among the lepers. There he used his extensive knowledge
of restorative surgery, and applied all he had learned in
London's emergency wards during the Blitz, to the
alleviation of some of the handicaps attaching to leprosy.
Leprosy usually resulted in horrifying mutilation of hands
and feet, and terrible disfigurement of the face, and
meant a life of ostracism and starvation. That was before
Paul Brand and his team of doctors, nurses, and labora-
tory specialists at the Christian Medical College at Vellore
gave lepers a new hope. By recognizing the latent power
in apparently useless hands, and by means of surgical
operations, these formerly doomed people were enabled
to live useful, productive lives. The author of this book
was a Dorothy Clarke Wilson. I returned the book reluctantly to the local library, and recommended it enthusias-
tically to all my friends.

A few weeks after my arrival in Orono I was introduced to the wife of a Methodist minister. Her husband
had retired from the ministry and they lived in Orono.
She was a charming, quietly spoken woman, with warm,
smiling eyes, and I liked her immediately. We were soon
deep in conversation, and she told me of her several
visits to England. I asked if she had relatives there, and

she told me she had many friends in England, where she had done research for her writing. 'You write books?' I asked. 'Oh, yes,' she answered smilingly. 'Under what name?' I queried. 'Oh, my own. Dorothy Clarke Wilson.' 'You wrote *Ten Fingers for God*?' I blurted out incredulously. I discovered that not only had this unassuming, completely unaffected woman written the book I admired so much—she had also written twelve other biographies, six novels, and seventy religious plays. Many of these books had been published, not only in America, but in Europe, Scandinavia, and Asia. Her novel *Prince of Egypt* was used as resource material for the film 'The Ten Commandments.' She had made four trips to India, and others to Palestine, Egypt, and England in order to do research for her books. One of her best-selling biographies is the story of Paul Brand's mother. Under the title of *Granny Brand* in America, and *Climb Every Mountain* in its original British edition, it tells the story of Evelyn Brand's ministering to the poor of India.

Dorothy Clarke Wilson has written the stories of courageous men and women, people of character and determination. Included among the subjects of her biographies are Susette La Flesche (*Bright Eyes*), an American Indian princess who spent her life fighting for the rights of her people, the Omaha Indians; Elizabeth Blackwell, the first woman in the world to become a full-fledged doctor, with an accredited degree; Dorothea Dix, the Maine woman who devotedly nursed wounded soldiers during the Civil War, and then by her labours in the cause of prison reform, and of humane treatment of the insane, won the admiration and reverence of the civilized world; Doctor Mary Verghese, the brilliant surgeon of Vellore, India, who, though paralysed from the waist down due to a car accident, helped others gain new strength and mobility; Hilary Pole, a courageous English girl stricken with myasthenia gravis, who though rendered completely helpless and her life tragically shortened, so rose above the devastating results of this dread

disease, that her brave spirit shone out, and was an
inspiration to all who came into contact with her. These,
then, are just a few of the people whose lives so impressed Dorothy Clarke Wilson by their courage, their
selflessness and tenacity, that she was compelled to
write about them.

One of my most prized possessions is a copy of *Ten
Fingers for God*, a gift from the author, and inscribed by
her. I feel privileged to have been able to know this
talented and likeable woman. Was this, too, accident or
design that I have been enabled to do so?

Having been born and brought up near the sea, any
suggestion of a trip to the coast is always welcomed with
enthusiasm by me. Therefore, when a friend of mine
suggested my accompanying her to Cape Split, on the
coast of Down East Maine, I was more than delighted to
do so. My friend, a poet and publisher, was to interview
Andrew Reiber, a fascinating former actor of over eighty
years of age. For eleven years Andrew had corresponded
regularly with the English novelist, poet, and essayist,
Vita Sackville-West. Andrew first wrote to Vita in March
of 1951, telling her that he had been reading and appre-
ciating her novels, poetry and essays for many years.
He requested, too, permission for a young American
friend of his, attending a school in Kent, to visit Vita's
home, Sissinghurst Castle, which dated from 1540.
Vita was intrigued by Andrew's letter, and his address,
'Windslip,' Cape Split, Maine, appealed, too, to her
romantic imagination. She replied to Andrew's letter,
and so began the unique friendship, which flourished and
continued until Vita's death in 1962. Through their
letters, Vita and Andrew discovered many shared interests, in books, in people, in dogs, and especially in
gardening matters, in which both were keenly interested.
Andrew sent Vita gifts of flower seeds, plants from his
garden at 'Windslip,' pine needle pillows, gardening
overalls, and patchwork quilts, as well as many other

gifts. How Vita must have enjoyed receiving these thoughtful, imaginative gifts from her overseas admirer!

The gardens at Sissinghurst are world famous, and were planted meticulously by Vita and her husband, diplomat and writer Harold Nicolson. Theirs was an unusual marriage, and is described vividly in the book *Portrait of a Marriage*, published in 1973 by their son, Nigel Nicolson. The young Vita's passion for Violet Trefusis (Keppel), daughter of Alice Keppel, King Edward VII's mistress, was at its height during the years 1918-1921. In spite of this, Vita and Harold achieved a loving and successful marriage. Vita's background was a colourful one. She was the only child from the union of Sackville West cousins. Her mother was Victoria, the illegitimate daughter of Lord Sackville, an English diplomat, and Pepita, a beautiful Spanish dancer. Through the marriage of Victoria to her cousin, Lionel, she became Lady Sackville, and thus Vita's ancestral home and birthplace was the magnificent Knole House in Kent. Her godmother was Queen Victoria. Vita wrote her grandmother's story in the book *Pepita*. Virginia Woolf was a friend, too, of Vita, and Vita was the model for Orlando in Virginia's 'biography' of that name.

Two most interesting and colourful people, then, were the reason for the visit to Cape Split; the talented woman writer from an illustrious English family, and the debonair actor from Maine. Her letters to him have now been immortalized in the book *Dearest Andrew*, edited by Dr. Nancy MacKnight, Professor of English at the University of Maine at Orono.

The morning in early November when we set out for Cape Split was almost springlike. When we reached the coast, the sight of the silvery ocean and the scent of the balsam firs which fringed the coastline were almost too breathtakingly beautiful for words. My friend and I walked in silence along the beach, drinking in the magical beauty and peace of the moment. We left reluctantly and

set out to find Andrew Reiber's home, 'Windslip.'
Passing the unpainted, weathered little houses, the
stacks of silver-grey lobster traps in their yards, we came
at last, just before the 'bar' or causeway to Cape Split
Place, to a mail-box clearly marked REIBER. We had
arrived. It was impossible to see a house. The tangled
shrubs, the tall grass, and two gnarled and twisted old
apple trees made it appear like the entrance to the
castle in 'Sleeping Beauty.' Eventually we found a path
leading to an open cavernous door. A large, thick-furred
dog waited for us expectantly there, not barking, but
leaping and whirling joyfully at the end of its chain,
and revealing excellent white teeth. We were able to see
the house now. It was a smallish, typical Maine Cape,
with clap-boards, once painted white, now almost hidden
behind a dense mantle of scarlet-leaved bushes reaching
almost to its eaves. We called tentatively into the darkness beyond the open door, 'Andrew, Andrew. Hello.'

A calm voice replied, 'Yes, I'm here,' and there on the
threshold stood an elderly man wearing a broad-brimmed
straw hat. Although he leaned on two canes there was no
impression of frailty about this man. He was well-built,
with powerful shoulders, and wore a navy blue crew-
necked sweater,with khaki trousers rolled up at the
ankles. His feet were bare. This was Andrew Reiber.
It was easy to see why he had been a successful stage and
film actor. He had an amazingly unlined face, with
finely moulded cheekbones and wide, clear blue eyes
and a firm mouth. His voice was resonant, his accent
almost English.

Brandy, the dog, released from its chain, tore into the
house and up the staircase. We passed through a dark
hall into a low-beamed dining room, and beyond that
into a sun-filled sitting room facing a meadow leading
down to the sea. The room was a treasure trove of mem-
ories; the old 'London Cries' prints, the shelves of books,
the silver-framed photograph of Vita, the albums of
photographs showing Andrew in stage and screen roles.

As we relaxed comfortably in the warm, sunny room, Andrew's mellow voice told us of his life. He was born in Louisiana, the son of a minister. As a child of five he mounted a tree-stump and recited poetry which he had made up. This feeling for words was the beginning of his desire to be an actor. His first theatrical part was in New Orleans at the Vieux Carré theatre. Later he was signed on by M.G.M. studios, and usually played supporting roles such as the hero's friend. The photographs in the many large albums we looked at showed Andrew as a debonair, handsome young man with a graceful posture and well-groomed hair. The elaborate stage sets in the photographs had been designed by Andrew's friend, the theatrical producer, Sir Walter Sinclair. It was in 1939 that he and Sir Walter bought 'Windslip.' They maintained five gardens there, and spent wonderful summers, with picnics, croquet tournaments, and scores of guests.

Whilst browsing through some theatrical albums I was particularly interested in one containing accounts of productions of the London theatres over the years. I was especially intrigued to find notices of two musical comedy productions in 1901 and 1902. These were 'The Earl and the Girl' and 'The Prince of Pilsen' at the Adelphi and Shaftesbury theatres, and were shows in which my husband's mother had appeared in London in those years. How amazing that I should find these accounts in a coastal town in Maine over three thousand miles away!

Andrew told us of his travels to various parts of the world, of his friendships with Paul Robeson, Sybil Thorndike, Katherine Cornell, and many other famous people. It was fascinating to re-live it all again with him. Leaving us to browse freely among his treasured books and albums, Andrew reached for his canes and said there were things he must do in the kitchen. Soon an unmistakable aroma permeated the air. Surely Andrew couldn't be boiling lobsters? After a while he appeared in the doorway to announce that luncheon was served. In the dining room we sat at the large, shining dark table.

There, indeed, were the lobsters, lying resplendent on a huge silver platter. A leather-covered box containing picks and crackers was nearby, and an egg cup containing melted butter was at each place setting. There were linen napkins, beautiful Chinese plates, lovely old silverware, and a centrepiece of fruit in a silver dish. A large pewter bowl filled with water was to be used as a finger bowl after the lobster. Andrew was the perfect host. He had thought of everything. There was even champagne. We drank a toast to Vita, and then set to work on the lobsters.

Later we returned to the sitting room for dessert, a superb creamy pudding on a large silver dish, which we ate from green Wedgewood 'lettuce' plates. Andrew informed us that this was a sea moss pudding, made from a type of sea-weed. It had a really delicate flavour, and we murmured our appreciation, wondering if Andrew had made it. He refused to be drawn, and instead mischievously showed us a quotation from a poem by Mona Van Duyn, 'Postcards from Cape Split': 'the man from across the bar / brought us a sea-moss pudding in a silver dish.'

All too soon the memorable day ended, and we left Andrew reluctantly. I kissed his cheek warmly, and we went out into the pale autumnal sunshine. Yet another bond had been forged, and I had made another new and special friend.

On a perfect early Summer afternoon, just two weeks before returning to England for good, I made a last visit to Indian Island. The sun danced on the water, and one or two brightly painted canoes lay on the river bank. The breeze was just enough to stir the leaves of the trees. A rather mangy dog eyed me suspiciously as I clambered down the steep slope, which led to a small wooden house at the foot of it. The only remarkable thing about the house was the name, painted in white on one of its walls — 'Wounded Knee.' I knocked on the door, and in a few moments it was opened by Madasa Sapiel, the elderly Indian woman whom I had met briefly a few weeks earlier at a meeting in Orono. She welcomed me warmly, and led the way into a small living room. It was hard to believe that this small, energetic lady, with high Indian cheekbones, expressive face, and intelligent, dark eyes, was seventy eight years old, but she assured me that she was, indeed.

Soon we were in animated conversation. Madas (most of her friends call her this) spoke nostalgically of Indian Island in the days when she was young. She could recall so vividly the beauty and peace of the island then, with great trees fringing the river's banks, and little paths snaking around the island. Indian men and women would sit outside their homes, weaving baskets, and chatting together. There were no fences, no door was ever locked, and every visitor was welcomed warmly.

Madas had been married three times and had had twelve children: three girls and nine boys. Two of her sons still live and work on Indian Island. One of them, 'Bobcat' Francis Glossian, I had met. 'Bobcat' is proud of his Indian heritage, and wishes for a return to the traditional values and beliefs of the past. His half-brother, Wally Pehrson, identifies with those who want to be part of the white man's world and its economy.

Madas told me that throughout her life she had earned a living using a variety of Indian skills. As a young girl she made baskets with her family, for sale at the coastal towns in Summer. For fourteen years she helped to support herself and her many children by dancing Indian dances in travelling shows. In addition to this, she worked for many years in the shoe factories across the river in Old Town. In her latter years, Madas became active in the militant Indian movement which asserted Indian autonomy and pride in a unique heritage. Madas told me, too, of her extensive travels to all parts of America. Her home was, she said, open always to Indians of all tribes, and from all parts of America and Canada.

Madas sometimes lapsed into the Indian language, which only a few of the tribe's elders now speak. She spoke regretfully of the lack of interest of today's young Indians in their culture or crafts, and of the harsh rebuffs she had encountered when she tried to teach the Indian language to the children on the island. She spoke of the great compassion and concern she felt for her people and their future.

'Sometimes,' she said sadly, 'I feel I just don't know my own people. I'm trying in all kinds of ways to help them, but how can you help a person if he doesn't want to be helped?'

In 1950, a single lane bridge was constructed which joined Indian Island to the mainland at Old Town. One reason for its construction was the increasing number of drownings while crossing the ice during the Spring and late Fall. The more important reason for building the bridge, however, was to make it easier for Indians to obtain education and employment, with this stronger connection between the island and the mainstream society. Many of the older Indians were regretful of the changes the building of the bridge had brought to the Penobscot tribe, including the increase of inter-marriage with the white people, and the consequent dilution of Indian blood. The younger Indians, however, mostly welcomed it.

When I told Madas I possessed a war club, carved for me by Senabeh Francis, a Penobscot Indian, a few weeks before his death in the winter of 1980, she told me that Senabeh had been a great friend of hers, and a great medicine man of the tribe. She said that very few were chosen as medicine men, that they were born such, and not made. Once, when she was very ill, Senabeh had appeared to her after his death, had touched her, and told her she would be well again the next day. She was, indeed, completely well when she awoke. On another occasion, a tall Indian chief appeared to her, sparks of electricity emanating from his finger-tips, leaving her feeling stronger and fitter when he left.

Uncannily, as Madas told me of these happenings in her calm, serene voice, it all seemed completely and absolutely natural. She spoke of her strong faith, the importance of the Catholic church in her life now, and of how she loved to go out of doors and throw her arms wide, and commune with the Great Spirit.

Eventually, it was time for me to leave. I did so reluctantly, knowing that I would probably never see Madas again. I felt so much richer for my visit to this very real and fascinating woman, a reminder of days when the Indians wandered freely and proudly the forests and lakes of Maine.

So many things I shall remember forever—the majestic hills silhouetted against the horizon, the conifer-edged lakes, the vast forests, the lupins growing wild in great patches of blue and pink, the golden lilies, the goldenrod and the purple asters. All these, growing in Maine in wild profusion, are to be found only in cultivated gardens in England. There are the birds: the lovely blue jay, the yellow grosbeak, the tiny humming bird, the chickadee, the phoebe and countless others. There is Maine's granite coast line, rugged and beautiful, with dark green conifers reaching right down to the edge of the sea. There are the small fishing harbours, the white wooden New England churches. How could I ever forget the splendour and glory of the Fall, or the dazzling whiteness of the snow against dark green conifers and the vivid blueness of the Winter sky?

There are the sounds of Maine, too, to be remembered: the whine of the chain saw in Summer and Fall as the prudent householder prepares his Winter fuel supply; the strident hooter, the clanging bell, and the rumble of the freight train as it passes by the foot of the Parsonage garden; the blue jay's raucous call, and the phoebe's plaintive note, the weird cry of the loon on the lake. Forever remembered, too, will be the carillon of the Catholic church at the top of the hill, pealing out its extensive repertoire ranging from, familiar hymn tunes to 'America the Beautiful,' 'Ramona,' and 'Stormy Weather'! And the church bell calling the congregation to worship at our church each Sunday; the people hurrying along the sidewalks to converge at the wide church doors; the singing in the sanctuary of well-loved hymns; and the sun streaming through the tall, many-paned windows.

There are the scents and flavours of Maine: the wood smoke from household stoves and fireplaces; the scent of the balsam fir in the forests; the perfume of lilacs and the wild flowers of Spring and Summer; the aroma of steak and hamburger barbecued out of doors; pop-corn prepared on a wood-stove and eaten salted and with melted butter, on a cold Winter's day in a Maine kitchen; pale yellow corn cobs picked fresh from the gardens, and cooked and served immediately on a huge platter. There are so many things that will remain forever in my memory.

What, though, shall I remember best — treasure most? Why, of course, the people; not so much the extraordinary few, but the character and colour and sheer niceness of the ordinary folk.

I enjoyed every moment of my life as a Maine-iac.

SELECT BIBLIOGRAPHY

Abbott, John S. C. *The History of Maine* (Boston: B. B. Russell, 1875).

Barnes, I. F. "A Safe Stronghold" (Plymouth, England: Latimer Trend, no date listed).

Baxter, James Phinney. *Sir Ferdinando Gorges and his Province of Maine* (Boston: The Prince Society, 1890).

— —. *The Trelawny Papers* (Portland, Maine: Maine Historical Society, 1884).

Burrage, Henry S. *The Beginnings of Colonial Maine* (Augusta, Maine: printed for the State, 1914).

Clifford, Harold. *Maine and Her People* (Freeport, Maine: Bond Wheelwright, 1957).

Coffin, Paul. *Memoirs of Paul Coffin, D.D.* (Portland, Maine: Maine Historical Society Collections, Vol. 4).

Day, Clarence. *Historical Sketch of the Town of Orono* (Orono, Maine: printed for the Town, 1956).

Dunnack, Henry E. *The Maine Book* (Augusta, Maine: printed for the State, 1920).

Eckstorm, Fannie H. *Old John Neptune and Other Maine Shamans* (Portland, Maine: Anthoenson, 1945).

Francis, Converse. *Lives of John Ribault, Sebastian Rale, and William Palfrey* (Boston: Little and Brown, 1845).

Gill, Crispin. *Plymouth: A New History*, vols. 1 and 2 (Newton Abbot, England; North Pomfret, Vermont: David and Charles, 1966, 1979).

Gilman, Stanwood and Margaret Cook. *Land of the Kennebec* (Boston: Brandon Press, 1966).

Holt, K. D. "Sir Ferdinando Gorges" (Plymouth, England: Latimer Trend, 1965).

Lanman, C. *Adventures in the Wilds of the United States and British American Provinces* (Philadelphia: J. W. Moore, 1856).

Levett. *A Voyage into New England, 1623-1624* (Portland: Maine Historical Collections, Vol. 2).

Macinnes, C. M. "Ferdinando Gorges and New England" (Bristol, England: University of Bristol, 1965).

Moulton, Augustus F. *Maine Historical Sketches* (Lewiston, Maine: Lewiston *Journal* Printshop, 1929).

Parkman, Francis. *The Jesuits in North America* (Boston: Little, Brown, 1905).

— —. *Pioneers of France in the New World* (Boston: Little, Brown, 1899).

Pike, Robert E. *Tall Trees—Tough Men* (New York: Norton, 1967).

Preston, Richard Arthur. *Gorges of Plymouth Fort* (Toronto: University of Toronto Press, 1953).

Ridlon, G. T. *Saco Valley Settlements and Families* (Portland, Maine: published by the author, 1895).

Rowse, A. L. *The Cornish in America* (London: Macmillan; New York: Scribners, 1969).

Speck, Frank G. *Penobscot Man* (Philadelphia: University of Pennsylvania Press, 1940).

Sprague, John Francis. *Sebastian Rale: A Maine Tragedy of the 18th Century* (Boston: The Heintzemann Press, 1906).

Springer, John S. *Forest Life and Forest Trees* (New York: Harper, 1851; Summersworth, New Hampshire: New Hampshire Publishing Company, 1971).

Sullivan, James. *History of the District of Maine* (Boston: printed by Thomas and Andrews, 1795; Hallowell, Maine: Glazier and Masters, 1839).

Thoreau, Henry. *The Maine Woods* (Boston: Ticknor and Fields, 1864).

Varney, George J. *A Gazeteer of the State of Maine* (Boston: B. B. Russell, 1886).

Verrill, A. Hyatt. *The Story of Plymouth* (England: Westaway Books, 1950).

Walling, R. A. J. *The Story of Plymouth* (Privately published, 1950).

— —. *History of Penobscot County* (Cleveland: Williams, Chase, 1882).

Williamson, William Durkee. *Annals of Bangor (History of Penobscot County)* (Hallowell, Maine: Glazier, Masters, 1832).

— —. *History of the State of Maine* (Hallowell, Maine: Glazier, Masters, 1839).

Willoughby, Charles C. *Antiquities of the New England Indians* (Cambridge, Massachusetts: Harvard University Press, 1943).

Wood, Richard G. *A History of Lumbering in Maine, 1820-1861* (Orono, Maine: University of Maine Press, 1935).

Photo composed in 12 point and 10 point English 18 on Compugraphic Execuwriter II. Printed on Atlantic Opaque, with Sundance Felt cover of Saddle Brown, and endpapers of Curtis Argyle text in Rose.

BOOKS BY PUCKERBRUSH PRESS

THE THOUSAND SPRINGS	short stories	Mary Gray Hughes
THE INVADERS	short stories	Marjorie Kaplan
DRIFTWOOD	Maine stories	Edward Holmes
CIMMERIAN	poems	Constance Hunting
AN OLD PUB NEAR THE ANGEL	short stories	James Kelman
DORANDO: A SPANISH TALE	novel	James Boswell edited by Robert Hunting
THE CROSSING	poems	Albert Stainton Rita Stainton
THE MOUNTAIN, THE STONE	short stories	Kathleen Kranidas
A DAY'S WORK	poems	Michael McMahon
A PAPER RAINCOAT	poems	Sonya Dorman
BEYOND THE SUMMERHOUSE	poem	Constance Hunting
A STRANGER HERE, MYSELF	short stories	Thelma Nason
farmwife	poem	lee sharkey
GREENGROUND- TOWN	short stories	Christopher Fahy
BETWEEN SUNDAYS	short narratives	Douglas Young
ONE TO THE MANY	poems	Anne Hazlewood-Brady
NOTES FROM SICK ROOMS	essay	Mrs. Leslie Stephen
TWO PLAYS	plays	Arnold Colbath
WRITINGS ON WRITING	essays	May Sarton
box of roses	poems	lee sharkey
DEAD OF WINTER	poems	Michael McMahon
DARKWOOD	poems	Michael Alpert
THE POLICE KNOW EVERYTHING	Downeast stories	Sanford Phippen
THE ROCKING HORSE	sermons for children	Douglas Young
IN A DARK TIME	anthology	Virgil Bisset and Constance Hunting, editors
LIGHT YEARS	poems	Roberta Chester
MY LIFE AS A MAINE-IAC	autobiography/history	Muriel Young